Northwestern University

Evanston, Illinois

Written by Torea Frey

*Edited by Adam Burns, Meghan Dowdell,
and Kimberly Moore*

Layout by Meryl Sustarsic

*Additional contributions by Omid Gohari,
Christina Koshzow, Chris Mason, Joey Rahimi,
and Luke Skurman*

ISBN # 1-4274-0104-7
ISSN # 1551-0536
© Copyright 2006 College Prowler
All Rights Reserved
Printed in the U.S.A.
www.collegeprowler.com

Last updated 8/14/08

Special Thanks To: Babs Carryer, Andy Hannah, LaunchCyte, Tim O'Brien, Bob Sehlinger, Thomas Emerson, Andrew Skurman, Barbara Skurman, Bert Mann, Dave Lehman, Daniel Fayock, Chris Babyak, The Donald H. Jones Center for Entrepreneurship, Terry Slease, Jerry McGinnis, Bill Ecenberger, Idie McGinty, Kyle Russell, Jacque Zaremba, Larry Winderbaum, Roland Allen, Jon Reider, Team Evankovich, Lauren Varacalli, Abu Noaman, Mark Exler, Daniel Steinmeyer, Jared Cohon, Gabriela Oates, David Koegler, and Glen Meakem.

Bounce-Back Team: Nicholas Lake, Jason Rosenbaum, Mike Saccone, and Evan Bradley.

College Prowler®
5001 Baum Blvd.
Suite 750
Pittsburgh, PA 15213

Phone: 1-800-290-2682
Fax: 1-800-772-4972
E-Mail: info@collegeprowler.com
Web Site: www.collegeprowler.com

How this all started...

When I was trying to find the perfect college, I used every resource that was available to me. I went online to visit school websites; I talked with my high school guidance counselor; I read book after book; I hired a private counselor. Sure, this was all very helpful, but nothing really told me what life was like at the schools I cared about. These sources weren't giving me enough information to be totally confident in my decision.

In all my research, there were only two ways to get the information I wanted.

The first was to physically visit the campuses and see if things were really how the brochures described them, but this was quite expensive and not always feasible. The second involved a missing ingredient: the students. Actually talking to a few students at those schools gave me a taste of the information that I needed so badly. The problem was that I wanted more but didn't have access to enough people.

In the end, I weighed my options and decided on a school that felt right and had a great academic reputation, but truth be told, the choice was still very much a crapshoot. I had done as much research as any other student, but was I 100 percent positive that I had picked the school of my dreams?

Absolutely not.

My dream in creating *College Prowler* was to build a resource that people can use with confidence. My own college search experience taught me the importance of gaining true insider insight; that's why the majority of this guide is composed of quotes from actual students. After all, shouldn't you hear about a school from the people who know it best?

I hope you enjoy reading this book as much as I've enjoyed putting it together. Tell me what you think when you get a chance. I'd love to hear your college selection stories.

Luke Skurman
CEO and Co-Founder
lukeskurman@collegeprowler.com

Welcome to College Prowler®

During the writing of College Prowler's guidebooks, we felt it was critical that our content was unbiased and unaffiliated with any college or university. We think it's important that our readers get honest information and a realistic impression of the student opinions on any campus—that's why if any aspect of a particular school is terrible, we (unlike a campus brochure) intend to publish it. While we do keep an eye out for the occasional extremist—the cheerleader or the cynic—we take pride in letting the students tell it like it is. We strive to create a book that's as representative as possible of each particular campus. Our books cover both the good and the bad, and whether the survey responses point to recurring trends or a variation in opinion, these sentiments are directly and proportionally expressed through our guides.

College Prowler guidebooks are in the hands of students throughout the entire process of their creation. Because you can't make student-written guides without the students, we have students at each campus who help write, randomly survey their peers, edit, layout, and perform accuracy checks on every book that we publish. From the very beginning, student writers gather the most up-to-date stats, facts, and inside information on their colleges. They fill each section with student quotes and summarize the findings in editorial reviews. In addition, each school receives a collection of letter grades (A through F) that reflect student opinion and help to represent contentment, prominence, or satisfaction for each of our 20 specific categories. Just as in grade school, the higher the mark the more content, more prominent, or more satisfied the students are with the particular category.

Once a book is written, additional students serve as editors and check for accuracy even more extensively. Our bounce-back team—a group of randomly selected students who have no involvement with the project—are asked to read over the material in order to help ensure that the book accurately expresses every aspect of the university and its students. This same process is applied to the 200-plus schools College Prowler currently covers. Each book is the result of endless student contributions, hundreds of pages of research and writing, and countless hours of hard work. All of this has led to the creation of a student information network that stretches across the nation to every school that we cover. It's no easy accomplishment, but it's the reason that our guides are such a great resource.

When reading our books and looking at our grades, keep in mind that every college is different and that the students who make up each school are not uniform—as a result, it is important to assess schools on a case-by-case basis. Because it's impossible to summarize an entire school with a single number or description, each book provides a dialogue, not a decision, that's made up of 20 different topics and hundreds of student quotes. In the end, we hope that this guide will serve as a valuable tool in your college selection process. Enjoy!

OMID GOHARI ◯ CHRISTINA KOSHZOW ◯ CHRIS MASON ◯ JOEY RAHIMI ◯ LUKE SKURMAN ◯
The College Prowler Team

Table of Contents

Introduction from the Author

Coming from the northwest corner of the United States, people are often befuddled when I tell them I go to Northwestern University. "Is that in Seattle?" they ask. Apparently, word hasn't reached Portland, Oregon yet about this ever-demanding, challenging, and intriguing school in suburban Chicago.

Most people already know—or think they know—about Northwestern: fairly small school, right outside of Chicago, excellent academic reputation … and, "Didn't Ross from Friends go there?" True, but to those on the inside, NU is so much more. It's a diverse school boasting six sub-schools that concentrate on everything from education to music to engineering. It's a campus open to discussing all aspects of contemporary global problems, and it's also our home.

Northwestern is often referred to as a jewel of the Midwest, and in the last 30 or so years, it has gained recognition as a leading research institution. The University has been entrenched in scandal over the death of a football player, and it has gotten into a lawsuit with the city of Evanston.

Behind the news and magazine articles, behind the historic legacies, and behind the campus tours, there is a throbbing pulse to Northwestern. As you leaf through the following pages, I hope you begin to discover the Northwestern that myself and my classmates all know: the living, ever-changing University, that is in a constant struggle to one-up itself and come out on top. You too can find the heartbeat of NU. You just have to be willing to feel for it. You can start by reading through this guidebook.

Torea Frey, Author
Northwestern University

By the Numbers

General Information

Northwestern University
633 Clark St.
Evanston, IL 60208

Control:
Private

Academic Calendar:
Quarter

Religious Affiliation:
None

Founded:
1851

Web Site:
www.northwestern.edu

Main Phone:
(847) 491-3741

Student Body

**Full-Time
Undergraduates:**
7,989

**Part-Time
Undergraduates:**
164

**Total Male
Undergraduates:**
3,852

**Total Female
Undergraduates:**
4,301

Admissions

Overall Acceptance Rate:
30%

**Early Decision
Acceptance Rate:**
44%

**Early Action
Acceptance Rate:**
Not offered

Regular Acceptance Rate:
30%

Total Applicants:
18,385

Total Acceptances:
5,434

Freshman Enrollment:
2,062

**Yield (% of admitted
students who actually enroll):**
38%

Early Decision Deadline:
November 1

Early Decision Notification:
December 15

Regular Decision Deadline:
January 1

**Regular Decision
Notification:**
April 15

Must-Reply-By Date:
May 1

Applicants on Waiting List:
1,572

**Applicants Accepting Place
on Waiting List:**
915

**Students Enrolled from
Waiting List:**
220

**Transfer Applications
Received:**
1,039

**Transfer Applications
Accepted:**
238

**Transfer Applications
Enrolled:**
143

**Transfer Application
Acceptance Rate:**
23%

SAT I or ACT Required?
Yes, either

**SAT I Range
(25th–75th Percentile):**
1320–1500

**SAT I Verbal Range
(25th–75th Percentile):**
650–740

**SAT I Math Range
(25th–75th Percentile):**
670–760

Freshman Retention Rate:
97%

**Top 10% of
High School Class:**
83%

**Common Application
Accepted?**
Yes

Application Fee:
$65

Admissions Phone:
(847) 491-7271

Admissions E-Mail:
ug-admissions@northwestern.edu

Admissions Web Site:
www.ugadm.northwestern.edu

Financial Information

Full-Time Tuition:
$35,064

Room and Board:
$10,776

Books and Supplies:
$1,548

**Average Need-Based
Financial Aid Package
(including loans, work-study,
grants, and other sources):**
$22,517

**Students Who Applied
for Financial Aid:**
49%

Applicants Who Received Aid:
85%

Financial Aid Forms Deadline:
February 1

Financial Aid Phone:
(847) 491-7400

Financial Aid E-Mail:
ug-finaid@northwestern.edu

Financial Aid Web Site:
ug-finaid.northwestern.edu

Academics

The Lowdown On...
Academics

Degrees Awarded:
Bachelor's
Master's
Post-master's certificate
Doctorate
First professional

Most Popular Majors:
20% Social Sciences
18% Journalism
14% Engineering
10% Visual/Performing Arts
 9% Psychology

Full-Time Faculty:
998

**Faculty with
Terminal Degree:**
100%

**Student-to-Faculty
Ratio:**
7:1

➜

Undergraduate Schools:

Kellogg School of Management

McCormick School of Engineering and Applied Science

Medill School of Journalism

School of Communication

School of Continuing Studies

School of Education and Social Policy

School of Music

Weinberg College of Arts and Sciences

Average Course Load:

Four classes per quarter

Class Sizes:

Fewer than 20 Students: 75%

20 to 49 Students: 17%

50 or More Students: 7%

Graduation Rates:

Four-Year: 85%

Five-Year: 93%

Six-Year: 93%

Special Degree Options

Accelerated program, cooperative education program, double major, honors program, independent study, internships, liberal arts/career combination, student-designed major, study abroad, teacher certification program

AP Test Score Requirements

Possible credit for scores of 4 and higher

Sample Academic Clubs

Alpha Chi Sigma (chemistry), Alpha Kappa Psi (business), Black Undergraduate Law and Business Society, Golden Key International Honor Society, Society of Professional Journalists

Best Places to Study

Deering Library, University Library, Norris University Center, and the Lakefill when it's nice out

Did You Know?

Though other schools participate in Primal Scream, Northwestern students mark the beginning of finals week with **Primal Streak**. This is when a group of students run scantily clad or naked from the Technological Institute to the Arch.

Students Speak Out On...
Academics

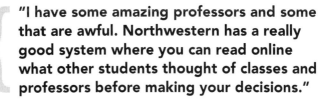

"I have some amazing professors and some that are awful. Northwestern has a really good system where you can read online what other students thought of classes and professors before making your decisions."

Q "There are the professors who are amazing, and then **there are some that are geniuses but can't teach**. I have only encountered one of them in my career here, but he's a nice guy and is always willing to explain things to you in office hours. Journalism is one of the best programs in the country, as are the music and theater programs. So it all depends."

Q "**It all depends on the department they are from**. Personally, I have been very happy with the political science and Euro history professors."

Q "Teachers are good; they will assist you if you like. It's a big school, so there are many grad students who have to tutor and answer questions for their degree; **there are always people to help**."

Q "For the most part, I have really liked all of my professors. Graduate students don't teach classes here, but they do work as teaching assistants. **It is important to get a good professor for your freshman seminar** because he or she becomes your freshman advisor. There are some really renowned teachers here, but it's usually hard to get into their classes as a freshman."

Q "If you network with your teachers, they **might be able to hook you up with a job** once you're out of school."

Q "**The professors, well, it depends**. Some are great, some not so much. But I would say the history, English, and political science departments have pretty solid professors. I hear fewer good things about those in math and science-related departments."

Q "Professors vary considerably, as I imagine they would at any other school. I've had some really great ones and some not-too-great ones. **Talk to older students about specific teachers** when you're interested in a class."

Q "It depends on what you take. Read the course and teacher evaluations before you register for a class with a certain professor, and ask people (sophomores in your dorm are good resources) what they thought of the professor. Also, **don't shy away from a professor just because they seem intimidating**—often, they are the most brilliant ones."

Q "The teachers are both good and bad. In my first year, I have had some great teachers and some really bad ones. When they're awful, it's mainly because **they're so smart they can't relate the material to the students**."

Q "The teachers are great. **It's cool to take a class with a teacher that's famous**. For the most part, classes are really interesting and the professors are awesome. Just check out course and teacher evaluations, and ask around before you take classes if you're unsure."

Q "I studied theater. **The theater program here is good if you want to study theater**, but know that you really want to take a lot of other classes. It is as far from a conservatory as you can get, and you'll be hard-pressed to find anyone who tells you if you're good or not, outside of student theater."

Q "Most **teachers are very friendly and engaging**. They enjoy getting to know students, so make the effort."

Q "Some classes yes, some no—probably true at any school. One big difference I noticed between college and high school was that **professors at NU are doing things in the 'real world' and are sometimes famous**, or at least well known in their field, which is cool and something you never find in high school. I think a decent portion of my interest in classes has been related to how much focus I choose to put on them."

Q "Northwestern features a pretty broad range of instructors, from crusty old professors to fresh-faced grad students. There's really no telling if your professor or TA will be any good, but I'd say at least 75 percent of my instructors so far have been at least tolerable. Some have been fantastic. The CTECs will usually give you a pretty clear picture of a class, at least from the scores if not the descriptions. **There are a lot of classes to be taken here, so seek out the ones you like**. Chances are, if it sounds interesting to you, it will be. If it sounds boring, it probably will be, too."

Q "For the most part, the teachers are very accessible and willing to help you if you ask. **I have never had a problem getting one-on-one time with a professor** if I took the time to ask for an appointment or went to office hours. I think it really varies; once you start taking classes in your major/minor, school gets a lot more interesting."

Q "The education at Northwestern is as good, and as hard, as you make it. Northwestern offers a variety of programs. **You'd be hard-pressed not to find something of interest and difficulty**."

Q "I really like the small classes because those professors will really try to get to know you, and they can spend more time working with you individually. The theater department is amazing, and every teacher I've had in theater has been incredible! **I can't say the same for some in other departments**."

Q "The teachers seem very experienced; they usually know what to expect of the students. Most of the teachers are good at explaining the material, too. I find almost all of my classes interesting because **they challenge me**."

Q "Being a music student, I don't really know much about what 'most' professors and classes are like, but I will describe the ones I know. MAB, where all the 'academic' music classes (like theory and music history) take place, is largely run by hip, young women (the coordinators for both the freshman and sophomore curriculums, as well as the undergraduate associate dean). However, that doesn't mean there are no bad teachers here, though the curriculum is good, the **TAs are sometimes incompetent, and you risk learning barely anything**."

Q "Most of the professors I've encountered like the classes they are teaching or are very interested in the subject, in general. But there are so many professors, it's pretty class/department specific. I do like most of my classes, but there always some that are going to be a real chore you have to force yourself out of bed for. **I really trust the course and teacher evaluations**; they haven't steered me wrong yet."

Q "The private teachers at Regenstein Music Hall are largely among the best in the world, especially the brass and percussion teachers. However, **a lot of the faculty members are aging** and refuse to admit that they are no longer qualified to teach and keep the money so that new teachers who can actually hear can't be hired."

The College Prowler Take On...
Academics

As with any school, professors at NU are hit or miss. You may have a class on Monday, Wednesday, and Friday with a professor as dry as week-old bread, but on Tuesday and Thursday, you may be sharing the classroom with a Tony Award-winning diva. Despite this variation, one thing's for sure: you'll never suffer through class with an unprepared graduate student forced to take the course on, so you always have access to instructors who are experts in at least some aspects of what they are teaching. Use the online ratings to help weigh whether or not a quarter of boredom is worth the resulting knowledge.

It's universally accepted that academics here are top-of-the-line. Though some students gripe, most come to Northwestern because they are ambitious and passionate about learning—even if they're not sure about what they want to concentrate on just yet. Take the time to schmooze with your professors, who are remarkably receptive to student initiative. Academics here are what you make of them. You have all the resources in front of you to begin your rise to the top of any chosen field. The theater and journalism programs are widely-regarded as the best in the country. But if you don't take advantage of the opportunities you're presented with, your experience likely will be sub-par. Go aggressively after what you want, and you'll be rewarded with knowledge, good grades, and excellent connections.

The College Prowler® Grade on

Academics: A

A high Academics grade generally indicates that professors are knowledgeable, accessible, and genuinely interested in their students' welfare. Other determining factors include class size, how well professors communicate, and whether or not classes are engaging.

Local Atmosphere

The Lowdown On...
Local Atmosphere

Region:
Midwest

City, State:
Evanston, Illinois

Setting:
Suburban

Distance from Chicago:
30 minutes

Distance from Milwaukee:
2 hours

Points of Interest:
Art Institute of Chicago
Navy Pier
Sears Tower

→

Shopping Mall:

Westfield Old Orchard
Shopping Center (Skokie)
34 Old Orchard Center
(847) 674-7070

Movie Theater:

Century 12 Theatre and
CineArts 6
1715 Maple Ave., Evanston
(847) 492-0123

Major Sports Teams:

Bears (football)
Blackhawks (hockey)
Bulls (basketball)
Cubs (baseball)
White Sox (baseball)

City Web Sites

www.cityofevanston.org
www.epl.org
www.visitchicagonorthshore.com

Did You Know?
5 Fun Facts about Evanston

- One of **the world's seven Bahai Temples** is within walking distance.
- Evanston lost its "**dry**" **status** by serving its first beer in 1972.
- The town claims it runs the "**World's Largest Garage Sale**" every year.
- **Tinker toys** were invented by an Evanston resident in 1914.
- Many people claim that the **ice cream sundae** was born in Evanston.

Famous People from Evanston:

John Cusack

Charlton Heston

Bill Murray

Students Speak Out On...
Local Atmosphere

> "**Evanston is not much of a college town. There are a lot of retirees, and things close early. But there's always Chicago, and Evanston really isn't that bad. We have a movie theater, lots of shopping, restaurants, and we're right on the lake.**"

Q "**Evanston's atmosphere is very nice**. Generally, the school, as a whole, does not have a good relationship with Evanston on political matters, but it's a great place to shop, eat, and just hang out. There are no other universities in Evanston, but there are several schools in Chicago."

Q "**Chicago is the best city in the world, as far as I am concerned**. It's big enough to have the feeling of a huge city, but its location in the Midwest and its size also makes it a very friendly, safe, clean city. Chicago has four other major universities and hundreds of smaller ones. Loyola, University of Chicago, University of Illinois at Chicago, and DePaul are all great places to hang out sometime if it's dead in Evanston."

Q "Evanston is a great town. There are a lot of renovations going on, and **there are new things popping up all of the time**."

Q "There are no other universities in Evanston, but Loyola is pretty close. **Chicago is such an awesome city**. I would stay away from some areas, but visit Michigan Avenue for great shopping. Go to the shows and the museums."

Q "There are plenty of universities in Chicago, and there is a **ton of stuff to visit downtown**. Also, trips to University of Illinois are lots of fun, as well as Indiana University and Wisconsin."

Q "**Evanston people don't really like Northwestern**. It's not a very college-oriented town. It's very pretty, though. There's good shopping and good restaurants, but not much else to do."

Q "It's right by Chicago, so Loyola and University of Chicago and some others are around, but there's not much interaction with them. **Chicago is great**. Go to Wrigley Field and the Neo-Futurarium; those are my favorite places. But visit downtown, too, it's really nice."

Q "**I don't think there are a lot of other university students hanging around Evanston**, but the areas that I'm in definitely are full of students. South Campus is nice because it's right near downtown Evanston. I don't see a lot of Evanston-Northwestern connections being made, except for necessary things like shopping, but I can't say that's really bothered me a lot. I'd like to get farther afield in Evanston and see more than just the downtown area, and I think that's worthwhile for everyone."

Q "Evanston is a city in transition from a little North Shore town to imitation Lincoln Park. But the influx of new, trendy businesses and restaurants, along with the movie theaters, has definitely brought more nightlife to the place. If you don't like it, though, **Chicago's just an easy El ride away, and there is no finer city** on this earth, if you ask me."

Q "Evanston is a good place to go to school. It's urban enough to be convenient for shopping and hanging out, but not too urban that it distracts from the campus. **I think it really strikes a good balance**."

Q "**The atmosphere seems somewhat laid-back**, though people are almost always doing something. There are several universities in Chicago, but they are spread out and require transportation to get to. Although Evanston does not have as high a crime rate as other places, it is still advisable to avoid traveling alone at night. Some good places to visit include the Cheesecake Factory and the Navy Pier. Also, Clarke's and Chipotle are great places in Evanston to get some food."

Q "Evanston is a very small, quaint place. The downtown is not that large, but the houses are all beautiful, and there are millions of amazing restaurants. It's right on the lake, which is beautiful, and you have the ability to go into Chicago, which is easy. **You really get the best of both worlds**; a suburban lifestyle or the big city."

Q "**Evanston is kind of strange, inhabitant-wise**. There are college students, old people, and lower-class people who are somewhat scary to the average NU student. Stick to well-lit places in downtown Evanston and on campus, and you should be okay. Also, visit the Bahai Temple in nearby Wilmette."

Q "I love Evanston! It's a suburb only a dozen or so miles north of Chicago (with excellent public transportation to downtown). It's a small town, with small shops; you have to go a bit out of walking distance for the nearest shopping mall, but it's a nice place if you have a car. There are a lot of restaurants for all tastes. There are a few small colleges and universities between us and Chicago, but we don't really pay much notice to them—they aren't exactly in the same town even. Stuff to stay away from: **don't bring a car until you're used to the city**, and if you have a car, be careful of parking—the city earns a huge chunk of its budget from parking tickets."

The College Prowler Take On...
Local Atmosphere

Northwestern and Evanston have a notoriously bad relationship—including a several-million-dollar lawsuit leveled against the University by the city. Though these tensions often run high, students are satisfied with the small town's offerings, particularly its restaurants. And for those looking to escape the sometimes small, snobbish feel of the north suburb, Chicago is a short train ride away—$1.75 grants you access to one of the great cultural centers of the world. Colleges in and around the city offer additional escape from NU and Evanston, should boredom set in.

Though politics may divide University people from townies, efforts are being made to bring the two together. Many local businesses offer discounts to students, which at least appeals to thrifty college students already thousands of dollars in debt. The town-gown split will be a hot topic for years to come, but it's not always apparent to students. Most of the time, the two populations peacefully coexist, but occasionally, when off-campus partying gets out of hand, gauntlets are thrown down. Be a good neighbor, try to steer clear of trouble, and take advantage of the dining capital of the North Shore, the cultural opportunities that are close at hand, and if nothing else, the beautiful shore of Lake Michigan.

The College Prowler® Grade on
Local Atmosphere: C+

A high Local Atmosphere grade indicates that the area surrounding campus is safe and scenic. Other factors include nearby attractions, proximity to other schools, and the town's attitude toward students.

Safety & Security

The Lowdown On...
Safety & Security

Police Phone:
(847) 491-3254
Campus Emergency: Dial 456

Safety Services:
Student escort service
SafeRide shuttles
University Police

Health Center:
633 Emerson Street
(847) 491-8100

(Health Center, continued)
Hours: Nurses – Daily 24 hours;
Practitioners – Monday/
Wednesday/Friday
8:30 a.m.–4:30 p.m., Tuesday/
Thursday 9:30 a.m.–4:30 p.m.;
Urgent Care Clinic – Saturday
9 a.m.–11:30 a.m.

Health Services:
Counseling and Psychological
Services (CAPS)
Health care

Students Speak Out On...
Safety & Security

> "I think people generally feel safe on campus. Certainly, there are events that cause alarm, but generally, people feel safe. However, going to school near a big city is evidently going to cause problems."

Q "Security has honestly been an issue as of late, but we have very little crime. I know that sounds odd, but all of a sudden we had a few assaults, so they are beefing up security more. That being said, **I often leave my door unlocked and do not feel uncomfortable doing so**. I rarely, if ever, feel unsafe at Northwestern, or in most of the surrounding area. Evanston is pretty tame, other than some somewhat aggressive panhandlers. We do have a lot of security options for students like the escort service, which will pick you up anywhere if you ever feel unsafe."

Q "Northwestern has its own police force; they have all the authority and privileges that any town police force has, except their main task is to enforce the laws here at NU. Although the campus can be pretty dark after sunset, I'd say **I always feel secure here, but then again, I'm a guy**; the women on campus might not share my sentiment."

Q "Security is not that much of a concern because the campus is in **Evanston, which isn't particularly crime-ridden**. The administration recently installed a bunch of new streetlights on campus."

Q "There have been some incidents on campus, but generally, **safety is high**. I have never been bothered, except for the occasional homeless person asking for change in downtown Evanston."

Q "I feel safe on campus, for the most part. The NU police are **always patrolling the streets**. However, there is not a great deal of lighting in certain areas, which is a negative. The escort service, which is supposed to be able to pick you up when it is late and you don't want to walk, is not all that efficient and sometimes they won't even be able to pick you up for two hours."

Q "This is a pretty safe campus because it's in the suburbs, but you have to remember that it is the first suburb north of Chicago. Evanston is a very diverse town, economically. The area surrounding the campus is really nice, but there are some bad areas of town. NU has its own police force in addition to the Evanston police. There are areas that you shouldn't walk alone at night, but for the most part, I feel safe. I must warn that **there have been some attempted sexual assaults** in the past few months, but the girls have gotten away because of police officers or other people in the area. This is highly out of the ordinary, and the University notified all the students in a bulk e-mail. The girls were walking in dark areas alone and pretty late at night. Also, I have never had a problem with theft in the dorm or anything like that."

Q "**Safety is not so hot, but they're working on it**. A lot of the campus is not well lit, but there is student escort that runs in the evening and will pick you up and take you to locations at or near campus. There is also a shuttle that runs in the evenings."

Q "There has been discussion about safety in the last few years. **People are mugged occasionally**, but I haven't heard of anyone being seriously attacked. If it's late, try to travel in groups and stay in well-lit areas. The police are around, but not necessarily when you need them."

Q "Most of the University area is pretty safe, but there are some very sketchy areas in Evanston, particularly the areas around Howard and the high school. In the daytime, though, you're basically safe anywhere. **Just be aware**."

Q "I would say that security on Northwestern campus is pretty good. There are lights and phones everywhere, and I have never had a problem. Also, there is a car service that runs from 9 p.m. to 2 a.m. so that you don't have to walk anywhere alone at night. **However, the surrounding area of the campus can be a bit shady**. For the most part, though, I think it's pretty good."

Q "Security and safety are well accounted for on campus. Most walkways are well lit and have emergency phones available. To prevent people from traveling alone, the University provides a student escort service at night. Depending on the dorm, theft usually isn't a problem. However, it is still advisable to lock your door when you are away since **theft happens occasionally**."

Q "I have heard of only a few serious incidents on campus. There are thefts, but if you are careful and close/lock windows on ground floors and follow common sense, there isn't too much of a problem. The reported number of assaults is small, and there is a great women's center and counselors on hand to help with all incidents (reported or not). In general, **I actually feel safe walking alone at night**."

Q "On campus, I feel completely safe, even in the middle of the night. There is adequate lighting and call-boxes are spaced regularly along all the pathways. **I rarely see non-students on campus late at night**. Off campus, it's a little less safe because Northwestern can't control the security level of the city. I try not to walk alone in Evanston after 10 p.m., but I have done it in the past without any resulting consequences."

Q "For the most part, security and safety are good on campus. **Just be smart**. Don't leave $20 sitting on the couch in your dorm lounge (Although, I know someone who did this for three days, and her money was still there when she came back.)"

Q "Well, we all know people periodically get mugged near campus or on the Lakefill, but I've never felt more than vaguely worried walking around, mostly because my mind tells me I should be concerned and not because I feel an actual threat. I guess I feel like the University's safety measures are nice and all, but we're all basically adults and **have a certain responsibility to look out for ourselves**. I've never felt that I deserved more than the University offers in terms of safety precautions. There are certainly enough locks on the doors."

Q "I always feel safe walking around on campus, even late at night. **It's still good to walk with someone if you can**, especially if you're going off campus."

The College Prowler Take On...
Safety & Security

Most people feel safe on campus, but several incidents in the past few years have been a cause for major concern. Racial epithets and threats to minority students destabilize the community, and attacks on female students leave some wary, to say the least. But for the most part, students report feeling very safe and applaud campus for its swift response to perceived security threats.

Even though it's so close to Chicago, Evanston is remarkably clean, safe, and well patrolled. However, small, isolated incidents still make the student population a little uneasy. For all the University can do, passing out silver whistles and verbally committing to more lights does not necessarily equal action. With a strong commitment to change, these problems should be resolved, but working out the deeper issues behind security breaches might be a better solution in the long run.

The College Prowler® Grade on
Safety & Security: C+

A high grade in Safety & Security means that students generally feel safe, campus police are visible, blue-light phones and escort services are readily available, and safety precautions are not overly necessary.

Computers

The Lowdown On...
Computers

High-Speed Network?
Yes

Wireless Network?
Yes

Number of Labs:
10

Number of Computers:
617

24-hour Labs?
No

Charge to Print?
5 cents for black and white;
75 cents for color.

Free Software:
Adobe Acrobat, Eudora,
Maple, Norton Antivirus,
Quicktime, RealPlayer,
Shockwave

Students Speak Out On...
Computers

> **"The network is good, the computer labs are never crowded, and almost all students have their own computer. I'd recommend bringing a PC, but it's not necessary to succeed here."**

Q "The network is nice—Ethernet is fantastic. I hate going home and having to use the dial up again. As far as computer labs go, they exist, but life is a lot easier if you have your own, especially because **our registration is online, and a lot of things revolve around e-mail**."

Q "**The computer labs are good**, although it can be frustrating when the printer is down in a lab or a bunch of computers aren't working. If you have one, or can afford one, you should bring it to school just because it is much easier to type a paper in your room than to travel to a lab and work there."

Q "Definitely bring your own computer, if just for convenience. **I have never seen the labs overcrowded, but it's a hassle** when you need to work on something at 3 a.m. and you have to go find an open lab. Also, having your own computer lets you keep in close contact with cross-campus friends."

Q "Bring your own computer, and make sure it has a network card installed. **The dorm connections and the connections around campus are super-fast**! I live off campus this year, so it was quite a shock to go back to modem. There are plenty of computer labs, but almost everyone brings a PC."

Q "I would say **if you have a computer bring it**, but if not, don't worry because the labs are nice."

Q "There are big computer labs and all-night Internet cafés, but yes, **bring your own computer**."

Q "**I would suggest that you bring your own computer**. I have a laptop, which I like, but isn't necessary. I think most of the dorms have computer labs, and the computers in the library are open. The network has fast connections and usually runs without any problems."

Q "I've never gone to a computer lab really, all I can say is the ones at the library for general usage are often being used. Yes, you should bring your own computer because it is useful for many things, and if you don't keep that in mind, **there's a general expectation that everyone does have a computer**. The Ethernet is lovely."

Q "Bring your own computer—period. **Your life will be easier**. Computer labs are bogus, and your connection is super-fast in the dorm room, so just bring one. They're ultra-convenient for pulling those all-nighters where you turn in your paper at the last second while you're still in your pajamas."

Q "I don't use computer labs much, but if you go during peak hours, they're usually full. Bringing your own computer is highly recommended because you'll be doing a lot of typing. Good high-speed connections and everything. Lately, **the University has been snooping around on people's computers**, though, so keep yourself covered."

Q "The computer network is fine. I have a laptop in my dorm room, and I have rarely, if ever, had a problem with my Internet connection. Since most students have their own computers, the computer labs are rarely packed. **Should I bring my own computer? Yes, definitely**."

Q "If you plan on writing a paper between 2 a.m. and 8:30 a.m., then you should bring your own computer, because the library is closed then. **I also highly recommend a laptop**. This way, you can write papers in the library if your dorm room is too distracting or your hallway too noisy."

Q "The computer network is fast, and the student home page has links to everything you need: course management, technical help, calendars, and transportation, and so on. Sometimes, the computer labs are crowded toward the end of finals week, but usually, there are several open computers throughout the rest of the school year. Definitely bring your own computer. It not only saves you the hassle of typing your papers in a lab, but also **lets you keep up-to-date with news and last minute e-mails**."

Q "I've never really been in the computer lab more than twice. I recommend having your own computer and a laptop instead of a PC. **It's nice to be able to take your laptop with you to the library** and get out of the dorm room or to take it home with you over breaks. It is also really nice in case the power goes out, since it will use its battery. If you are in the middle of writing an important paper, you can continue to do so while everyone else is freaking out."

Q "**Bringing your own computer is not only an option— it's a necessity**. The connection is reliable and fast, but you can't download music unless you're really sneaky (they monitor you)."

Q "I was without a computer my first week on campus—get a computer and Ethernet access. **It's really hard to live without it**. The computer labs are highly accessible, according to my experience, and the connection is fast. I have not had a problem accessing a computer when I need to or having to go out of my way to access one."

The College Prowler Take On...
Computers

A computer isn't necessary at NU, but it sure is handy. Although there are no 24-hour computer labs per se, once you learn the ins and outs of the University, it's fairly easy to find an open computer at any time of the day or night. Labs in the journalism school are fully equipped for desktop publishing, and the schools of music and communication offer state-of-the-art editing for CD and video production. Wireless connectivity is rather limited, so don't feel obligated to get a laptop. But on a practical basis at Northwestern, the socially challenged often find it easier to communicate over Instant Messenger from a dorm room than by picking up the phone and dialing out. Fast Ethernet connections enamor even the most computer-clueless student, and even if you've never been hip to the Web before, you'll be savvy in no time. Still, be prudent, or you'll be banished from the network if you're caught downloading too much too fast.

Disregard the school's recommendations for computers unless you are in a highly specialized field or you're willing to splurge. A bare-bones computer that can be hooked up to the Internet is an absolute must, and don't be surprised if your roommate has thousands of dollars invested in his setup. Computers are a matter of leisure and allow students the luxury of doing their dirty work in the comfort of pajamas. It's a competitive school, and often the only time to let your hair down is at the dorm or your apartment. Find a computer that fits your needs and rely on the labs only in the case of emergency—and don't forget to download AIM.

B-

The College Prowler® Grade on

Computers: B-

A high grade in Computers designates that computer labs are available, the computer network is easily accessible, and the campus' computing technology is up-to-date.

Facilities

The Lowdown On...
Facilities

Student Center:
Norris University Center

Athletic Center:
Crown Sports Pavilion,
Drysdale Field, Lakeside Field,
McGaw Memorial Arena,
Recreation Center, Rocky Miller
Park, Tennis Center

Campus Size:
231 acres

Libraries:
5 on the Evanston campus,
and 3 on the Chicago campus,
available to all students
(8 in total)

Popular Places to Chill:
Friends' apartments
Lakefill
Lisa's Café
Norris University Center

What Is There to Do on Campus?

Between classes, work, and extracurriculars, there's no shortage of entertainment at NU. Enjoy one of the hundreds of student theater productions at Shanley Pavilion, share a cup of joe at Lisa's Café, catch a flick on A&O Productions, or throw a pot at Artica Studios.

Movie Theater on Campus?

Yes, McCormick Auditorium

Bowling on Campus?

No

Bar on Campus?

No

Coffeehouse on Campus?

Yes. Willie's Too at Norris University Center, Tech Express at the Technological Institute, Lisa's Café at Slivka Residential College, Plaza Café at University Library, Crowe Café at Crowe Hall.

Favorite Things to Do

Students can play beach volleyball, sail, bike ride, inline skate, attend plays in Shanley Pavilion, or catch a show at the Century Theater.

Students Speak Out On...
Facilities

"For the most part, I think the facilities are pretty good. Norris could be updated, but I find that most everything is up to par."

Q "Facilities here are fantastic, although **it depends on what you're interested in and what school you're in**. The Technological Institute, which houses all engineering and most science classes, is the third largest building in the world under five stories (behind the Kremlin and the Pentagon, I think). The facilities are state-of-the-art. Our library, aesthetically, leaves a little something to be desired, but it is very functional."

Q "The student center is okay, but definitely not one of the best features here. It has an eating area, a study area, and a game room, but that's it. **The athletic center has been remodeled and is a definite plus**. The library is huge and has everything you would ever need."

Q "Computer labs are nice, and most of the classrooms are state-of-the-art and air conditioned. **A few buildings are still living in the '60s**, but the school is constantly remodeling and updating the facilities."

Q "SPAC is the main athletic center for working out. **It is really nice with lots of equipment**, an indoor track, basketball courts, racquetball courts, and tennis courts. There are two other gyms on campus, too."

Q "**The student center, Norris, is nice and usually busy**. I'm not really sure about the computer facilities since I have my own, but I have no trouble using computers in the library labs when I need to."

Q "There are a lot of gyms, and they seem really nice. The library is intimidating but useful, and **you can find a computer anywhere**."

Q "I like the pool at SPAC a lot, and I think the athletic facilities are generally in good shape. **Norris is bland, but useful**."

Q "Great athletic facilities. The pool is huge and well maintained. **Most of the computer facilities are in good order, but you may have to hike a bit** to get to one. Norris is cool. Get a meal plan with lots of Munch Money so you can eat there. All in all, there are a lot of good facilities."

Q "**I find the campus facilities to be more than adequate for most students' needs**. The main gym, SPAC, was just renovated and is a great place to work out. The student center is also a wonderful resource. It houses all of the student organizations, as well as the best dining hall food on campus, a small bank, comfortable lounge chairs, and computer stations that are great for group meetings or taking a nap between classes."

Q "The computers in Tech and the library are pretty convenient. SPAC is nice, and Patten and Blomquist are good—**smaller and less crowded** if you just want to play basketball or something."

Q "Supposedly, SPAC is a great place to exercise, but it is rather inconvenient for people on the south end of campus. There is Blomquist, however, and it is a decent gym in the middle of campus. The computer labs are very nice. They have high-powered computers with up-to-date software. The student center is very nice, too, because it has **convenient shops for food, books, video rentals, and postage**. Most of the buildings are nice on campus, except the Music Administration Building. It is old and needs repairs."

Q "**The facilities on campus are really nice**. The theaters are beautiful, the gym is loaded with up-to-date machines, and the student center has pretty much anything you would possibly need."

Q "**The student center is crappy**. It has a nice food court, bookstore, and video rental place, but that's really all that's useful in it to the average student. There are two main places to work out: one old, crappy, non-air conditioned, smelly, small gym (which is generally populated by sorority girls), and one huge health-spa-like gym that is populated largely by Evanston residents during the day. I've never been there at night."

Q "The facilities are nice. They have gyms south, north, and in between. **The student center is constantly being renovated**. There are theater venues all over South and Middle Campus. I have nothing to complain about except that the music buildings could use a little bit of attention, especially the practice rooms—they definitely need some sound proofing."

The College Prowler Take On...
Facilities

In recent years, Northwestern has experienced a building boom—unfortunately, most of these buildings are for offices or specialty departments, not for undergraduates. The campus is a hodgepodge of different architecture, ranging from the classic University Hall to the hulking behemoth of University Library to the clean, futuristic McCormick Tribune Center. The Sports Pavilion and Aquatic Center is a huge, modern workout facility that draws varsity athletes and out-of-shape nerds alike. Norris, the student mecca, draws perennial complaints, but with the economy in a downturn, it's unlikely to get renovated any time soon.

Despite some shortcomings, most people find the facilities serviceable. Norris is always packed with students looking for everything from a study space to a late-night snack. Computer labs are adequate, and exercise spaces dot the campus. There may not be a bowling alley or a bar on campus, but NU students find plenty to do with their time—including supporting a thriving student theater scene and a strong academic presence.

B

The College Prowler® Grade on
Facilities: B

A high Facilities grade indicates that the campus is aesthetically pleasing and well-maintained; facilities are state-of-the-art, and libraries are exceptional. Other determining factors include the quality of both athletic and student centers and an abundance of things to do on campus.

Campus Dining

The Lowdown On...
Campus Dining

Meal Plan Average Cost:

Northwestern offers unlimited meal plans, weekly allotted meals, and strictly structured blocks ranging from $3,822–$4,368 per year

Freshman Meal Plan Requirement?

If living in University housing, freshmen are initially assigned to a 13-meal-per-week plan, but this can be changed.

Places to Grab a Bite with Your Meal Plan:

1835 Hinman Dining Hall

Food: Grill, soup, pasta, salad bar, cereal bar, ice cream bar

Location: 1835 Hinman

Hours: Monday–Friday 7:30 a.m.–9:45 a.m., 11:15 a.m.–1:15 p.m., Saturday 10:45 a.m.–1:30 p.m., Sunday 11 a.m.–2 p.m., 4:45 p.m.–7 p.m.

Allison Dining Hall

Food: Grill, soup, pasta, salad bar, cereal bar, ice cream bar

Location: Allison Hall

Hours: Monday–Friday
7:30 a.m.–9:45 a.m.,
11:15 a.m.–1:15 p.m.,
4:45 p.m.–6:45 p.m.

Crowe Café

Food: Pre-made sandwiches, snacks, Seattle's Best coffee

Location: Norris

Hours: Monday–Thursday
8 a.m.–4:45 a.m.,
Friday 8 a.m.–3 p.m.

Einstein Bros. Bagels

Food: Coffee, bagels, salads, soups

Location: Second floor of Pancoe Life Sciences Pavilion

Hours: Monday–Thursday
8 a.m.–4:45 a.m.,
Friday 8 a.m.–3 p.m.

Elder Dining Hall

Food: Grill, healthy, hot line, desserts

Location: Elder Hall

Hours: Monday–Friday
7:30 a.m.–9:45 a.m.,
11:15 a.m.–1:15 p.m.,
4:45 p.m.–6:30 p.m.

Foster-Walker Complex Dining Hall East

Food: buffet-style, tofu stir-fry, hot line, salad bar, soups, cereal, desserts

(Foster East, continued)

Location: Foster-Walker Complex, east wing

Hours: Monday–Thursday
7:30 a.m.–10:45 a.m.,
11:15 a.m.–4:45 p.m.,
5:15 p.m.–7:30 p.m.,
8 p.m.–11:30 p.m.,
Friday 7:30 a.m.–10:45 a.m.,
11:15 a.m.–4:45 p.m.,
5:15 p.m.–7:30 p.m.,
Saturday 7:30 a.m.–9:45 a.m.,
10:45 a.m.–1:30 p.m.,
4:45 p.m.–7 p.m.,
Sunday 11 a.m.–2 p.m.,
4:45 p.m.–7 p.m.

Foster-Walker Complex Dining Hall West

Food: Made-to-order burgers, burritos, salads, and sandwiches, cereal, desserts

Location: Foster-Walker Complex, west wing

Hours: Monday–Thursday
7:30 a.m.–10:45 a.m.,
10:45 a.m.–1:15 p.m.
4:45 p.m.–7p.m.,
8 p.m.–11:30 p.m.
Friday 7:30 a.m.–10:45 a.m.,
10:45 a.m.–1:15 p.m.
4:45 p.m.–7p.m.,
Saturday 7:30 a.m.–9:45 a.m.,
10:45 a.m.–1:30 p.m.,
4:45 p.m.–7 p.m.,
Sunday 11 a.m.–2 p.m.,
4:45 p.m.–7 p.m.

Lisa's Café

Food: Coffee, pastries, juices, sub sandwiches

Location: Slivka Residential College

(Lisa's Café, continued)

Hours: Monday–Thursday
10 a.m.–2 a.m.,
Friday 10 a.m.–7 p.m.,
Saturday 11 a.m.–7 p.m.,
Sunday 12 p.m.–2 a.m.

Plaza Café

Food: Seattle's Best coffee,
sushi, sub sandwiches,
smoothies

Location: 1970 Campus Drive

Hours: Monday–Thursday
8:30 a.m.–11 p.m.,
Friday 8:30 a.m.–3 p.m.,
Saturday 12 p.m.–4 p.m.,
Sunday 5 p.m.–11 p.m.

Sargent Dining Hall

Food: Grill, soup, pasta, salad
bar, cereal bar, ice cream bar

Location: Sargent Hall

Hours: Monday–Friday
7:30 a.m.–10:45 a.m.,
10:45 a.m.–4:45 p.m.,
4:45 p.m.–8 p.m.,
Saturday 7:30 a.m.–9:45 a.m.,
10:45 a.m.–1:30 p.m.,
4:45 p.m.–7 p.m.,
Sunday 11 a.m.–2 p.m.,
4:45 p.m.–7 p.m.

Tech Express

Food: Coffee, pastries, juices,
sub sandwiches

Location: Technological
Institute

Hours: Monday–Thursday
8 a.m.–6:30 p.m.,
Friday 8 a.m.–3 p.m.

Willard Dining Hall

Food: Grill, soup, pasta, salad
bar, cereal bar, ice cream bar

Location: Willard
Residential College

Hours: Monday–Friday
7:30 a.m.–9:45 a.m.,
11:15 a.m.–1:15 p.m.,
4:45 p.m.–6:30 p.m.

Willie's Food Court

Food: Small food court
featuring a grill, stir-fry,
sandwiches, Willie's Too
(coffee), wraps

Location: Norris

Hours: Monday–Thursday
11 a.m.–7 p.m.,
Friday 11 a.m.–3 p.m.,
Saturday 11 a.m.–3 p.m.,
Sunday 12 p.m.–7 p.m.

Student Favorites:

Lisa's Café

Sbarro's in Norris

Off-Campus Places to Use Your Meal Plan:

None

24-Hour On-Campus Eating?

No, but Foster-Walker Hall
offers a late-night meal until
11:30 p.m.

Students Speak Out On...
Campus Dining

{
"The food on campus is generally good. The dining halls are all pretty much the same and offer a wide variety of foods at each meal. Elder and Allison halls are probably the best in terms of environment."

Q "Food really isn't bad. **It just gets a little tedious**. At first, I was really excited about all the possibilities in the dining halls, but they get old after a while. However, we also have Norris University Center, which provides more palatable choices, and you can use part of your meal plan for that. Overall, it isn't bad."

Q "The student union also has a large eating area, **but that is generally used by older students living off campus**, who eat during the day when they are on campus."

Q "Dorm food stinks, and food at the Norris Student Center isn't much better. Yet, **Evanston is known as the dining capital of the North Shore**, so there are tons of restaurants off campus that are awesome."

Q "Here, **you cook for yourself**."

Q "**Food on campus is not good**. Sorry, but there's no way around that. Once you are off the meal plan, there are plenty of good restaurants in the surrounding town of Evanston to be taken advantage of."

Q "Food is **good; it's like cafeteria food, but better**. It changes daily in the main union, but there are lots of different places to eat."

Q "The food is not great. **The student center has good food, but they rip you off**."

Q "**Food? Well, it is dorm food**! There are two different types of meals plans: normal and flex. The normal meal plan allows you a certain number of meals in the dining halls on campus. The dining halls aren't that bad, and they are pretty much all the same."

Q "**The Allison Dining Hall on South Campus is my favorite**. There is a good variety of food. I was on the normal meal plan first quarter. Now, I'm on flex, which gives me a bunch of Bonus Bucks to eat at Norris University Center. Norris has better food, and if you don't use your entire Bonus Bucks, then you can get drinks and food at the end of the quarter."

Q "The food is not terrible, and from what I hear from my friends when they visit me, it's better than the food where they are. **I highly recommend getting on the flex meal plan**, which allows you to eat at Norris. There are more choices and better choices for vegetarians."

Q "People complain about the food, but I get the feeling people do that everywhere. **Personally, I like the food**."

Q "The food is what you would expect. **The dining halls aren't bad but can get repetitive**. If you live on South Campus, there are lots of places in Evanston that can give you a break from the dining halls—BK, Giordano's, Jimmy John's, and many more."

Q "The food is not good—Norris is slightly better, I think, but then again, maybe it's just exciting because it's different; I did get very tired of it after two years. Alison has nice big windows, everyone talks about Sargent, but I've only been there once and was not blown away. **I think you just have to grit your teeth and deal with it** until you move off campus."

Q "**Stay away from 1835 Hinman. It's deadly**. Allison and Norris have pretty good food. I recommend the block plan."

Q "It varies quite a bit from place to place. Stay away from Foster-Walker. **Most people agree that Sargent has the best food on campus**. Norris is generally good, although it's very expensive. Try a few places out and see what you think. Chances are you'll end up going to whichever place is closest to you."

Q "Dining halls vary, but the best place for food on campus is Norris. **Also, Lisa's Café is a good place to spend Bonus Bucks on grocery items**."

Q "Although others claim there is a difference, I think the food seems the same at each dining hall. The only difference is the presentation or space at particular dining halls. Some of the food is really good. Some of it is decent. And some of it is not so good. Usually, there is something that tastes pretty decent. Look out for special occasions because, **sometimes, the dining halls go all out on food**, usually with a theme (for example, gourmet night, Christmas)."

Q "Dining halls are fun because you will always have a friend you can eat with. Allison Hall has a huge salad bar, which is fantastic. Normally, I eat at Norris because the selection is huge, and their hours are more conducive to a busy schedule. Campus dining isn't terrible, but it's not that great. **But, hey, we're here for the education not the food**."

Q "**Eat at Norris, the student center**. You have to get on a special meal plan to do it often, but it's worth it. Other than that, Sargent is the best dining hall, but it's up North. Allison is the best on South Campus, and Hinman is the worst on South Campus."

Q "The food is edible, and **the chefs try hard**. They will attempt any dish you want, really. They are always looking for suggestions and trying them. Service at Norris leaves a lot to be desired, but the food is decent for college food."

The College Prowler Take On...
Campus Dining

There are no rave reviews, but not a lot of people complain about toxic food or becoming physically ill from campus dining. Each dining hall has unique characteristics, but all share a common thread. The food, though prepared by friendly chefs, gets tedious after a quarter—spaghetti and pizza day after day. Most students eventually convert to a meal plan that allows them to eat at Norris or the numerous coffee joints, which add a little more variety to the sometimes monotonous fare.

In general, the consensus seems to be that food at Northwestern is passable, but not pleasurable. It is more expensive than cooking for yourself, and the quality is not top-of-the-line. However, the school's food service does make an effort to please their patrons and will cater to your every need—if you ask for assistance. When you're tired of cereal and bagels every night, venture into Evanston, heralded the "dining capital of the North Shore."

The College Prowler® Grade on

Campus Dining: B-

Our grade on Campus Dining addresses the quality of both school-owned dining halls and independent on-campus restaurants as well as the price, availability, and variety of food.

Off-Campus Dining

The Lowdown On...
Off-Campus Dining

Restaurant Prowler:
Popular Places to Eat!

Blind Faith Café
Food: Healthy, breakfast
525 Dempster St.
(847) 328-6875
www.blindfaithcafe.com
Price: $6–$10
Hours: Monday–Thursday
9 a.m.–9 p.m.,
Friday 9 a.m.–10 p.m.,
Saturday 8 a.m.–10 p.m.,
Sunday 8 a.m.–9 p.m.

Burger King
Food: Fast food
1829 Dempster St.
(847) 733-8740
Price: $3–$7.
Hours: Sunday–Thursday
6 a.m.–12 a.m., Friday–
Saturday 6 a.m.–1 a.m.

Carmen's of Evanston Pizzeria
Food: Pizza
1012 Church St.
(847) 328-0031
Price: $10–$15

(Carmen's, continued)

Hours: Sunday–Thursday
10 a.m.–10 p.m.,
Friday 11 a.m.–11 p.m.

Clarke's

Food: Breakfast, burgers

720 Clark St.

(847) 864-1610

Price: $7–$10.

Cool features: Breakfast all day

Hours: Daily 7 a.m.–12 a.m.

Chipotle

Food: McBurritos

711 Church St.

(847) 425-3959

www.chipotle.com

Price: $6–$8

Cool Features: Though a subsidiary of McDonald's, this little Mexican joint draws a large student crowd.

Hours: Daily 11 a.m. –11 p.m.

Flat Top Grill

Food: Stir-fry

707 Church St.

(847) 570-0100

www.flattopgrill.com

Cool Features: Create your own stir-fry

Price: $9–$14

Hours: Monday–Thursday
11 a.m.–10 p.m., Friday–
Saturday 11 a.m.–11 p.m.,
Sunday 11 a.m.–9:30 p.m.

Giordano's

Food: Deep dish Chicago-style pizza, Italian

500 Davis St.

(847) 475-5000

www.giordanosflorida.com

Cool Features: All pizza is half-price after 5 p.m. Monday nights for dine-in orders.

Price: $8–$22

Hours: Monday–Thursday
11 a.m.–11 p.m., Friday–
Saturday 11 a.m.–1 a.m.,
Sunday 12 a.m.–11 p.m.

Joy Yee's Noodles

Food: Chinese

521 Davis St.

(847) 733-1900

www.joyyee.com

Cool Features: Bubble drinks

Price: $4–$12

Hours: Monday–Thursday
11:30 a.m.–10 p.m., Friday–
Saturday 11:30 a.m.–10:30 p.m.,
Sunday 12 p.m.–10 p.m.

Las Palmas

Food: Mexican

817 University Pl.

(847) 328-2555

Cool Features: In-house band

Price: $7–$16

Hours: Monday–Friday
11 a.m.–10 p.m.
Saturday 11 a.m.–11 p.m.,
Sunday 12 p.m.–10 p.m.

Mandarin House

Food: Chinese and Korean
819 Noyes St.
(847) 869-4344
Price: $4–$10
Hours: Tuesday–Thursday
11 a.m.–9:30 p.m., Friday–
Saturday 11 a.m.–10 p.m.,
Sunday 4 p.m.–9:30 p.m.

Mt. Everest

Food: Indian and Nepali
630 Church St.,
(847) 491-1069
www.mteverestrestaurant.com
Cool Features: All-you-can-eat
lunch buffet for about $8
Price: $8–$16
Hours: Monday–Thursday
11:30 a.m.–2:30 p.m.,
5 p.m.–9:30 p.m.,
Friday 11:30 a.m.–2:30 p.m.,
5 p.m.–10 p.m.,
Saturday 12 p.m.–3 p.m.,
5 p.m.–10 p.m.,
Sunday 12 p.m.–3 p.m.,
5 p.m.–9:30 p.m.

Noyes St. Café

Food: Italian, Greek, American
828 Noyes St.
(847) 475-8683
Cool Features: Full-service bar
Price: $6–$10
Hours: Monday–Thursday
11 a.m.–10 p.m.,
Friday 11 a.m.–11 p.m.,
Saturday 8 a.m.–11 p.m.,
Sunday 8 a.m.–10 p.m.

Potbelly Sandwich Works

Food: Sandwiches, shakes,
smoothies, cookies
630 Davis St.
(847) 328-1800
www.potbelly.com
Cool Features: Delivery
Price: $7–$12
Hours: Daily 11 a.m.–11 p.m.

Sherman Restaurant

Food: Italian
1740 Sherman Ave.
(847) 328-2050
Price: $5–$9
Hours: Daily 7 a.m.–9 p.m.

Trattoria Demi

Food: Italian
1571 Sherman Ave
(847) 332-2330
Price: $6–$10
Hours: Monday–Thursday
11 a.m.–9 p.m., Friday–
Saturday 11 a.m.–10 p.m.,
Sunday 12 p.m.–9 p.m.

Trio Atelier

Food: Bistro-style
1625 Hinman Ave.
(847) 733-8746
www.trio-restaurant.com
Price: $12–$27
Hours: Wednesday–Thursday
5:30 p.m.–9 p.m.,
Friday 5:30 p.m.–10 p.m.,
Saturday 5 p.m.–10 p.m.,
Sunday 5 p.m.–9 p.m.

Other Places to Check Out:

Baja Fresh
Cozy Noodle & Rice
Dave's Italian Kitchen
D & C Hot Dogs
Dozika
Kafein
Lucky Platter
Lulu's
New Japan Restaurant
Olive Mountain
Steak & Shake
Tapas Barcelona
That Little Mexican Café
Thai Sookdee Restaurant
Vive La Crepe

Grocery Stores:

Dominick's Finer Foods
1910 Dempster St.
(847) 866-9026

Dominick's Finer Foods
1763 West Howard St.
(773) 761-7022

Jewel-Osco
1128 Chicago Ave.
(847) 869-7950

Osco Drug
1630 Sherman Ave.
(847) 475-6256

Best Breakfast:

Clarke's

Best Chinese:

Mandarin House

Best Healthy:

Blind Faith Café

Best Pizza:

Giordano's

Best Place to Take Your Parents:

Trio Atelier

Off-Campus Dining

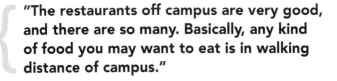

"The restaurants off campus are very good, and there are so many. Basically, any kind of food you may want to eat is in walking distance of campus."

Q "The restaurants in Evanston are fantastic. **We are known as the 'dining capital of the North Shore' for a reason**. There is almost every kind of food you can imagine, from Chinese to vegan to steakhouses. There is also a little café near campus which serves fantastic breakfast food all day called Clarke's. It's a chain, but a darn good one."

Q "The restaurants off campus are many and wide-ranging. **Basically, whatever you would want is within a short walk**. I personally enjoy a Mexican place called Las Palmas, but really, whatever you are looking for will be available at a low price. Evanston is known for this."

Q "**Flat Top, Chipotle, Dave's Italian Kitchen, and D & C Dogs are all good places to eat**. And if worse comes to worst, you can always chill at the 24-hour Burger King or Steak & Shake."

Q "There are a ton of restaurants off-campus, **and most give a small discount for Northwestern students**."

Q "The restaurants off campus are good and **a lot of them deliver**. Giordano's and Carmen's have great deep dish pizza. Kafein is a great, trendy coffee shop where you can get coffee, milkshakes, sandwiches, and desserts. Potbelly's has the best sandwiches and really good milkshakes."

Q "Panera is a soup, salad, sandwich, and bakery place that rocks. There's Flat Top, which is a stir fry bar where you can create unlimited stir fries. Chipotle has awesome burritos. **There aren't many restaurants on campus, but it isn't a far walk into Evanston**. Plus, there are so many good restaurants downtown, too many to list."

Q "The restaurants in Evanston are good. It depends on what kind of food you like, but Flat Top Grill is really good and so is Las Palmas Mexican. **Plus, there is anything you want in downtown Chicago**."

Q "No restaurants on the actual campus, but just off campus there are tons of great places. **They're mostly near south campus**. Let's see … Clarke's, Las Palmas, Cozy Noodle, Flat Top, and Chipotle are all favorites with students."

Q "Evanston is considered the 'Dining Capital of the North Shore,' so there is a good variety of nice restaurants. Some are too expensive, but you can get Indian, Thai, Italian—pretty much anything. And everybody likes Chipotle burritos. **Unfortunately, not many places are open late**."

Q "Many good restaurants nearby, which often tempt you to spend money you do not have and **avoid dining hall food**. I like Olive Mountain, Joy Yee's, Thai Sookdee, Mt. Everest, The Lucky Platter, Blind Faith Cafe, and of course Giordano's on Monday night—there are more that I can think of, but food is definitely something to take advantage of in Evanston."

Q "**Food in town is hit or miss.** There's half off pizza at Giordano's on Mondays. Joy Yee's is good. Baja Fresh and Clarke's are also favorites. You can always take the El train into Chicago."

Q "Evanston has a huge variety of great food, much of it quite inexpensive. For Italian, try Trattoria Demi. Giordano's has famously delicious stuffed pizza. For Mexican food, Chipotle offers great burritos, and Las Palmas and That Little Mexican Cafe have everything else. Mt. Everest offers delicious and modestly-priced Indian and Nepalese cuisine. Blind Faith Cafe is a vegetarian restaurant that's a little pricey but definitely recommended. Dozika and New Japan offer some very good sushi and other Asian cuisine. And if you just want a sandwich, Potbelly and Panera are both cheap and very tasty. Vive le Crepe is a cool place that just opened, and it is fairly cheap as well. **There is much good food to be enjoyed**."

Q "There's no shortage of restaurants in Evanston. Just about **every ethnicity is represented**, and a wide price range. My favorites are Tapas Barcelona and Lulu's."

Q "**The restaurants in Evanston are awesome**. Carmen's Pizza is the best and Giorodano's has half-price pizza night on Monday's. Mount Everest has great Indian food, and Clarke's is always great for a yummy Charlie Brownie Sundae. (The most amazing and huge brownie sundae in town!)"

Q "Every Monday is Giordano's half-price pizza night—you must go at least once to understand. **It's the best pizza in the world, and you can eat enough to be quite full on less than $5 once a week**. Good for dates: Trattoria Demi: cute little Italian bistro-ish place. I recommend the lasagna spinaci. Good 'fast' food': Potbelly Sandwich Works (Try the chocolate chip oatmeal cookies, they're to die for. Also the pizza sub is my personal recommendation). Joy Yee's Noodles is the best not-national chain Asian food I've ever had. It's not terribly expensive, the service is super-fast, the food is fabulous, and there is a wide range from 'typical' to 'really out there,' and they have these great teas and fresh fruit smoothies that you can get tapioca bubbles in (very hip trend—must try)."

The College Prowler Take On...
Off-Campus Dining

The sheer volume and variety of tasty vittles right on NU's doorstep earns consistently high marks from students. There may be no restaurants on campus to speak of, but a mere five-minute walk leads you to a global culinary adventure. Clarke's, a cozy hangout, offers food for all palates and breakfast all day long. Burger King is the only 24-hour restaurant within close proximity, and Sherman, a late-night cashier, is an NU legend. Other popular spots are Chipotle and Flat Top Grill, a hop, skip, and a jump from campus, and good date fare.

Getting off-campus every once in a while is a good idea, and Evanston's restaurants make it that much better. Stray a little from well-known haunts to discover quaint eateries like Blind Faith Café or the Noyes St. Café. Northwestern's student government also created a database of Evanston restaurants that gives ratings, menus, and other vital info. Consult this Bible of sorts, grab a friend, and get ready to be pleasantly surprised.

The College Prowler® Grade on

Off-Campus Dining: A-

A high Off-Campus dining grade implies that off-campus restaurants are affordable, accessible, and worth visiting. Other factors include the variety of cuisine and the availability of alternative options (vegetarian, vegan, Kosher, etc.).

Campus Housing

The Lowdown On...
Campus Housing

Undergrads Living on Campus:
65%

Number of Dormitories:
20

Number of Residential Colleges:
10

Best Dorms:
Kemper Hall
Allison Hall
Willard Residential College

Worst Dorms:
Bobb Hall
Foster-Walker Complex

➔

Dormitories:

584 Lincoln
Floors: 4
Total Occupancy: 36
Bathrooms: Shared by floor
Coed: Yes
Room Types: Single, double
Special Features: Main lounge, TV lounge, kitchenette

600 Lincoln
Floors: 3
Total Occupancy: 45
Bathrooms: Shared by floor
Coed: Yes, single-sex floors
Room Types: Single, double
Special Features: TV room, study room, rec room, vending

626 Emerson (Phi Mu Alpha)
Floors: 4
Total Occupancy: 32
Bathrooms: Shared by floor
Coed: No, men only
Room Types: Single, double
Special Features: Main lounge, rehearsal room, TV lounge, rec room, kitchenette

720 Emerson St. (Sigma Alpha Iota)
Floors: 3
Total Occupancy: 26
Bathrooms: Shared by floor
Coed: No, women only
Room Types: Single, double

(720 Emerson St., continued)
Special Features: Main lounge, kitchenette, rec room, study lounge

1835 Hinman
Floors: 5
Total Occupancy: 229
Bathrooms: Shared by Floor
Coed: Yes, single-sex suites
Room Types: Single and double suites
Special Features: Lounge, TV room, library, computer room, kitchenette, vending, carpeted halls, dining services

2251 Sheridan
Floors: 3
Total Occupancy: 48
Bathrooms: Shared by floor
Coed: Yes, single-sex floors
Residents: Transfer students
Room Types: Single, double
Special Features: Main lounge, TV lounge, study lounge, G.R.E.E.N. House

Allison Hall
Floors: 4
Total Occupancy: 355
Bathrooms: Shared by wing
Coed: Yes, single-sex wings
Room Types: Double, triple
Special Features: Main lounge, floor lounges, rec room, TV lounge, study room, vending, carpeted halls, dining services

Bobb Hall

Floors: 4

Total Occupancy: 245

Bathrooms: Shared by wing

Coed: Yes, single-sex wings

Room Types: Double, triple

Special Features: Main lounge, floor lounges, rec room, study room, vending

Elder Hall

Floors: 3

Total Occupancy: 287

Bathrooms: Shared by the wing

Coed: Yes, single-sex wings

Residents: Freshmen

Room Types: Single, double

Special Features: Main and floor lounges, TV room, rec and study rooms, vending, dining services

Foster House

Floors: 3

Total Occupancy: 48

Bathrooms: Shared by floor

Coed: No, men only

Room Types: Single, double

Special Features: Main lounge, TV room, rec room, vending

Foster-Walker Complex

Floors:4

Total Occupancy: 627

Bathrooms: Shared by 4

Coed: Yes, single-sex clusters

Room Types: Single, quad

(Foster-Walker, continued)

Special Features: Lounges, rec room, kitchenette, air conditioning, services for students with disabilities, vending, carpeted halls, dining services, Healthy Living Unit (substance-free), and Interfaith Living and Learning Community

Goodrich House

Floor: 4

Total Occupancy: 45

Bathrooms: Shared by floor

Coed: No, women only

Room Types: Single, double

Special Features: Living room, TV room, built-in furniture, recreation room

Hinman House

Floors: 3

Total Occupancy: 42

Bathrooms: Shared by floor

Coed: Yes, single-sex floors

Residents: Freshmen

Room Types: Double

Special Features: TV room, rec room, vending, North Side Coffee Company

Kemper Hall

Floors: 4

Total Occupancy: 177

Bathrooms: Shared by suite

Coed: Yes, single-sex suites

Residents: Upperclassmen

Room Types: 16 Single suites or 11 double suites

(Kemper Hall, continued)

Special Features: Main lounge, TV lounge, classroom, kitchenettes, air conditioning, carpeted halls

Lindgren Hall

Floors: 4

Total Occupancy: 37

Bathrooms: Semi-private

Coed: Yes, single-sex floors

Room Types: Single, double

Special Features: Living room, TV room, rec room, kitchenette, vending

McCulloch Hall

Floors: 5

Total Occupancy: 243

Bathrooms: Shared by wing

Coed: Yes, single-sex wings

Room Types: Double, triple

Special Features: Main lounge, floor lounge, rec room, study room, vending

North Mid-Quads Hall (NMQ)

Floors: 4

Total Occupancy: 85

Bathrooms: Shared by wing

Coed: Yes, single-sex wings

Room Types: Single, double

Special Features: TV room, rec room, kitchenette, vending

Rogers House

Floors: 3

Total Occupancy: 50

(Rogers House, continued)

Bathrooms: Semi-private

Coed: No, women only

Room Types: Single, double, triple

Special Features: Spacious living room, high-ceiling communal room, rec room, TV room

Sargent Hall

Floors: 4

Total Occupancy: 152

Bathrooms: Shared by floor

Coed: Yes, single-sex by floor

Room Types: Single, double

Special Features: Large main lounge, rec room, kitchenette, vending, dining services

South Mid-Quads Hall (SMQ)

Floors: 4

Total Occupancy: 88

Bathrooms: Shared by wing

Coed: Yes, single-sex by wing

Room Types: Single, double

Special Features: TV room, rec room, kitchenette, vending

Residential Colleges:

Ayers College of Commerce and Industry (CCI)

Location: 2324 Campus Dr.

Floors: 4

Total Occupancy: 164

Bathrooms: Shared by wing

Coed: Yes, single-sex wings

(Ayers, continued)

Room Types: Single, double

Special Features: Living room, TV lounge, rec room, seminar room, computer lab, library, kitchenettes, vending

Communications Residential College (CRC; East Fairchild)

Location: 1855 Sheridan Rd.

Floors: 4

Total Occupancy: 107

Bathrooms: Shared by suite

Coed: Yes, single-sex suites

Room Types: Single and double suites

Special Features: Main lounge, seminar room, computer room, radio studio, video editing facility, darkroom, vending

College of Cultural and Community Studies

Location 2303 Sheridan Rd.

Floors: 5

Total Occupancy: 39

Bathrooms: Shared by floor

Coed: Yes, by floor

Room Types: Single, double, triple

Special Features: Panelled living room, TV lounge, recreation room, classroom, computer room, kitchenette

Humanities Residential College (Chapin)

Location: 726 University Pl.

Floors: 3

(Humanities, continued)

Total Occupancy: 70

Bathrooms: Shared by wing

Coed: Yes, single-sex wings

Room Types: Single, double

Special Features: Lounge, library, computer room, kitchenette, vending machines

International Studies Residential College (ISRC; West Fairchild)

Location 1861 Sheridan Rd.

Floors: 4

Total Occupancy: 103

Bathrooms: Shared by suite

Coed: Yes

Room Types: Single and double suites arranged by language

Special Features: Main lounge, TV room, seminar room, activities area, computer room, kitchenette, vending machines

Jones Fine and Performing Arts Residential College

Location 1820 Sheridan Rd.

Floors: 4

Total Occupancy: 118

Bathrooms: Shared by suite

Coed: Yes, by suite

Room Types: Single, double

Special Features: Main lounge/ performance room, computer rooms, art and craft studios, dance studios, practice rooms, kitchenette, vending machines

Public Affairs Residential College (PARC)

Location: 1838 Chicago Ave.

Floors: 4

Total Occupancy: 113

Bathrooms: Shared by suite

Coed: Yes, single-sex by suite

Room Types: Single and double suites

Special Features: Main lounge, seminar room, carpeted halls, computers, kitchenette, vending,

Shepard Residential College

Location: 626 University Pl.

Floors: 5

Total Occupancy: 180

Bathrooms: Shared by wing

Coed: Yes, single-sex wings

Room Types: Single, double, triple

Special Features: Main lounge, TV/VCR lounge, rec room, computer room, music room, library, classroom, vending

Slivka College of Science and Engineering

Location: 2332 Campus Dr.

Floors: 4

Total Occupancy: 137

Bathrooms: Shared by suite

Coed: Yes, single-sex suites

Room Types: Single, double

Special Features: Kitchenette, small lounge, music room, study lounge, rec area, Lisa's Café, the Discovery Room

Willard Residential College

Location: 1865 Sheridan Ave.

Floors: 4

Total Occupancy: 290

Bathrooms: Shared by the wing

Coed: Yes, single-sex wings

Room Types: Single, double, triple, quad

Special Features: Main lounge, TV/VCR lounge, "smart" lounge, computer room, library, billiard room, vending, dining services

Women's Residential College (WRC; Hobart House)

Location: 630 Emerson St.

Floors: 2

Total Occupancy: 50

Bathrooms: Semi-private

Coed: No, women only

Room Types: Single, double, triple

Special Features: Living room, computer lab, library, TV room, kitchenette, vending

Room Types:

Singles, doubles, triples, quads, and suites

Bed Type

Twin extra-long (39" x 80"); some bunk beds

Cleaning Service?

Excellent. There's a cleaning staff present five days a week. They keep all common areas neat and clean.

What You Get

Varies from dorm to dorm, but all are furnished with bed and desk. You also get Ethernet connection and free campus phone service.

Did You Know?

Northwestern's residential college system is a part of University housing that **receives special funding** and offers thematic activities to residents.

Around 900 undergraduates choose to live with their **fraternities or sororities**.

Students Speak Out On...
Campus Housing

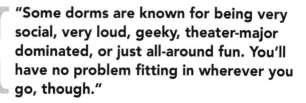

"Some dorms are known for being very social, very loud, geeky, theater-major dominated, or just all-around fun. You'll have no problem fitting in wherever you go, though."

Q "The dorms really depend on where you want to live. We have all sorts of dorms—suites, singles, doubles, triples, quads—with varying social scenes and room sizes. The northern dorms tend to be a little more party-oriented, being near the frats. **The southern dorms are a little quieter, but not boring**. Some dorms (the engineering residential college) are really tame and quiet."

Q "**The dorms vary**. I think Allison, Elder, and Bobb are the best. I would avoid Foster-Walker and any of the residential colleges. But it all depends on what you want. If you want a party dorm, then Elder, Bobb, or Allison are good, but if you want something more laid-back, then Foster-Walker or Hinman might be more for you."

Q "**Dorms are okay**. Try to get into the bigger ones like Allison, 1835, Elder, Bobb, or McCulloch. Those are the party dorms. Stay away from residential colleges because they are very cliquish. If you want to pay a pretty penny for the really nice dorms, try for Slivka or Kemper."

Q "If you're a math or science type, you'll want to live on the north part of campus. If you're more liberal and artsy, live on the south. **Allison is probably the best dorm to live in as a freshman**, but NMQ and SMQ and Willard aren't bad."

Q "Foster-Walker is known for being anti-social, but it's also said that people there have a lot of sex, so I guess it's up to the individual to weigh that. I think residential colleges do help people get to know each other and have sort of a community feel. The downside of a good dorm is **it can be too easy to stick with the people in your dorm and never get out**. Lots of people like Willard; it seems to appeal to many types of students."

Q "The dorms vary as widely as the food. **Most of the residential colleges are cool**, and offer more of a communal atmosphere with fun activities and handy resources. Jones is great! In terms of pure niceness, Kemper is probably the best dorm, but I've only been in there once. I like the atmosphere in Willard and Allison. I try to avoid Bobb, McCulloch, and PARC at all costs."

Q "I think there's a dorm to suit every kind of person. If you are overly social, enjoy binge drinking 3–4 nights a week and plan on rushing, then live in Bobb-McCulloch or somewhere else up north, if you're a little more bohemian and value a more low-key environment, then live on South Campus. The residential colleges are a great way to meet people. There are a lot of dorm-sponsored events to take part in, and **you get to know your whole dorm**."

Q "**Most dorms are pretty good**. Hinman has smaller rooms, but they have lounges in each suite. Allison is very nice with decent-sized rooms. Kemper is a cool place to live as an upperclassman because it has suites with six bedrooms, a bathroom, and kitchenette."

Q "**Avoid Bobb if you don't like drinking and extremely loud people**. The residential colleges are the best way to feel part of a group as opposed to the other large dorms which don't really have bonding activities."

The College Prowler Take On...
Campus Housing

Northwestern wages its own civil war every year: North Campus versus South Campus, with Foster Street representing the great divide. Generally, North Campus attracts engineering kids and students in the hard sciences, and South Campus is populated more by theater and journalism majors—originally anchored in the proximity to certain academic departments. While some will say North attracts more partiers, wild dorm life can be found in every corner of campus—if you look hard enough. There is also a split between dorms and residential colleges, catered more toward students with specialized interests.

It is quite possible that some of your best friends throughout college will be the ones you meet during the first couple of days in the dorms. There is little rhyme or reason to selecting housing. It's difficult to know the reputations of various places during the spring of your senior year in high school. However, NU students are easygoing, and regardless of stereotypes, there will be a wide variety of people living just seconds from you, no matter where you stay. There are options for everyone, from pocket-protector-sporting math students to free-loving liberal artists. Overall, the dorms are comfortable, if a little cramped, and most students are satisfied enough to live on campus for at least two years.

B

The College Prowler® Grade on
Campus Housing: B

A high Campus Housing grade indicates that dorms are clean, well-maintained, and spacious. Other determining factors include variety of dorms, proximity to classes, and social atmosphere.

Off-Campus Housing

The Lowdown On...
Off-Campus Housing

Undergrads in Off-Campus Housing:
35%

Average Rent For:
Studio Apt.: $500–$700
1BR Apt.: $700–$900
2BR Apt.: $1,300–$2,100

Best Time to Look for a Place:
Late winter or early spring

Popular Areas:
Clark Street
Foster and Maple
Ridge and Davis

For Assistance, Contact:
Student Affairs,
Off-Campus Housing
www.northwestern.edu/offcampus/index.html
(847) 467-2748

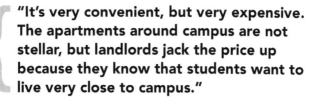

Students Speak Out On...
Off-Campus Housing

{ **"It's very convenient, but very expensive. The apartments around campus are not stellar, but landlords jack the price up because they know that students want to live very close to campus."**

Q "**Off-campus housing is a little on the expensive side, but it is accessible to campus**. Most people live a few blocks from campus, making it very easy to walk or bike to class."

Q "Off-campus housing is plentiful. I have lived off campus the last two years; **it was not hard to find a place, and the rent has been pretty good**. Also, you can choose a place based on where most of your classes are to reduce walking and what not."

Q "I recommend moving across the border into Chicago when you live off campus. **I pay about $200 less a month than most of my friends.**"

Q "Housing is pretty convenient, although the apartment search can be stressful. **It's helpful if you're friends with a graduating senior with a nice apartment**. Some freshmen choose to move off campus, but most choose to stay on campus for at least another year. Living in a dorm on campus is the best way to meet people. Living in an apartment denies you that opportunity."

Q "Off-campus housing is not difficult to find and is pretty close to campus. **There are a lot of parties off campus**. Most people live off campus junior and senior year."

Q "Housing is convenient and nearby, but can be expensive. Also, it is not always in the best condition. **Landlords like to take advantage of college students**."

Q "There's quite a bit of housing near campus, but it is obviously more expensive than what's farther away. **I don't know if it's worth it yet**, but I'm going to assume that it is on the basis of having a chance to cook and having my own bathtub. I always thought of living in an apartment as a part of the whole college experience."

Q "I'm staying in the dorms for my third year. It's closer to campus, your friends, and your classes. **I personally don't think it's worth the hassle to get an apartment**."

Q "Get an early start when finding a lease—the apartments around here fill up very quickly. There are a lot of nice ones, though, depending on how far from campus you're willing to go. You will probably end up **spending less for an apartment with roommates than you will in a dorm**, so go for it if you're interested."

Q "I totally recommend off-campus housing. You've finally become adjusted after your freshman year and off-campus housing is a **logical and fun next step as you prepare for the real world**. It's a more independent way of living, but you will learn a lot and make some great friends."

Q "Housing off campus can be a real pain sometimes. It's not uncommon for seniors to stay in residential colleges all four years. Apartments can be expensive in Evanston, and the **laws are kind of stacked against tenants**, but NU tries hard to ease the experience. They even currently released an apartment guide that shows how to go about renting an apartment."

Q "A lot of apartment buildings in Evanston are fairly old—and not necessarily well-kept. Go through your place with the landlord before you move in so you can account for damages that aren't yours. **Be smart, and don't go in blindly**—or else you'll end up paying $500 a month to live in a dumpy two-room shack with three other people, like I did."

The College Prowler Take On...
Off-Campus Housing

Like any college town, Evanston landlords tend to take advantage of the naiveté of students. And, being a wealthy suburb of Chicago, housing prices are inflated—but it's still less expensive than University housing. It is, by no means, mandatory to get your own apartment, but many students choose to do so after their sophomore year and are happy with the choice. Realize, however, that there are certain caveats that come with the responsibility of apartment rental.

Freedom comes at a price—and near NU, it's astronomical. Small apartments for an average of $1,250 a month are not everyone's idea of paradise. However, if you can stand to commute, living further from the familiar gives you a bit of a price break. With a little research, affordable, comfortable houses and apartments can be found, but beware of deals that sound too good to be true—they probably are. Hash out your lease well in advance, go through the apartment for possible damage before you move in, report anything suspect to your landlord early, and get ready to party!

The College Prowler® Grade on

Off-Campus
Housing: C+

A high grade in Off-Campus Housing indicates that apartments are of high quality, close to campus, affordable, and easy to secure.

Diversity

The Lowdown On...
Diversity

Asian American:	**Native American:**
16%	Less than 1%
African American:	**White:**
6%	61%
Hispanic:	**Unknown:**
6%	6%
International:	**Out of State:**
5%	75%

Political Activity

College Democrats, College Republicans, Green Party

Gay Pride

One student group, Rainbow Alliance, addresses gay issues.

Economic Status

Relatively high-end, considering this is a pricey, private institution.

Minority Clubs

Alianza (Hispanic/Latino), For Members Only (black undergraduate organization), South Asian Students Alliance, Thai Club, Korean American Students Association, and many more

Most Popular Religions

Mostly Christianity or Catholicism, as well as Judaism.

Students Speak Out On...
Diversity

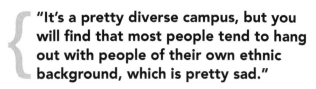

{ **"It's a pretty diverse campus, but you will find that most people tend to hang out with people of their own ethnic background, which is pretty sad."**

Q "I'm not going to lie, **diversity is a little on the weak side**."

Q "**The campus is very diverse**. There's a wide mix of people of all races."

Q "Diversity is a huge issue at Northwestern. **The campus is extremely open-minded and liberal**, so it's not hard to find groups of friends hanging out who are black, white, Indian, Asian, Latino, gay, straight, or whatever. Diversity is always included within campus-wide dialogue."

Q "The campus is **very diverse but very cliquish**."

Q "It's pretty diverse, I would say. **I think diversity is one of Northwestern's greatest strengths**."

Q "I'd say **we have a lot of white people and Asians**, but the black population is small."

Q "I think the campus is pretty diverse, although most people are very wealthy. That's unfortunate, but most **people aren't really snobs, just a little out of touch**."

Q "This is the most diverse place I have ever been to. There are places on campus where I, as a white male, am definitely the minority. Fortunately, **everybody gets along just fine**."

Q "In past years, there were a few unfortunate incidences on campus. During Winter and Spring Quarters two years ago, racial epithets were written on some peoples' doors—including a graphic depiction of someone being hung, drawn on a black student's door. Despite these aberrations, **most people are very accepting of differences**. It's too bad the unenlightened few can peg a university as stubborn and out-of-date. The administration, student body, and now the FBI are joining up to make sure the people who perpetrated the hate crimes are rightfully punished."

Q "NU is not nearly as diverse as my high school, but it's not as white as I thought it would be either. **North Campus seems more diverse than South Campus**."

Q "**I think the squirrel population on campus is more diverse than our student body**. Campus is primarily whites and Asians. It's pitiful."

Q "Pretty diverse. I came from a very diverse high school, so to me it seems really white on campus, but **there seem to be a lot of Asian students**. For a top-tier university, I guess it's more diverse than one might expect."

Q "The perceived diversity of campus really depends on what you're involved in. **As a sociology major, I find my classes to be incredibly diverse**, but I think that this is more the exception than the rule. Overall, campus is more diverse than I had expected it to be. There are a wide array of active student organizations that all host a number of events each year to reach out to the entire Northwestern community. I think if you want diversity then it's there, you just might have to go out and find it."

Q "According to the administration and The *Daily*, NU is not diverse enough. I think it's pretty diverse. **Sometimes groups self-segregate**, though."

Q "I would say it's diverse, and so is Chicago. **There are lots of culture clubs and events**. The groups are definitely a good place for all students, and the events are open to everybody. And it seems like all the ethnic groups get along really well (as in, no friction between groups)."

Q "The campus is pretty diverse. **It is not uncommon to hear several languages being spoken**. On the other hand, the campus is still dominated by Caucasians."

Q "The campus is extremely diverse as far as what locations people come from and their socioeconomic backgrounds. Racially, there are still many more white people than others. However, **there is a minority presence which cannot be overlooked**. There's a lot to be learned from others that Northwestern is sensitive to in creating a diverse student body."

The College Prowler Take On...
Diversity

For many students coming from privileged backgrounds, NU is the epitome of diversity—hey, there's lots of Asians, right? If you're from a more racially-integrated, urban area, though, you realize the fairly homogenous character of the student body. Despite some disheartening acts in past years, people at NU are relatively accepting and open-minded about differences, real or perceived. Campus is fairly united, with most people being economically well-off and extremely well-educated.

If you're a minority, you may sometimes feel out of place, but there are lots of cultural clubs that thrive on campus. There is also a sense of intellectual curiosity among students that pushes many to seek knowledge about other cultures and ways of life. Unfortunately, the ignorance of some can overshadow the sophistication of many, as occasional, scattered hate crimes still occur. Although Northwestern stresses diversity and acceptance of one and all, there is unspoken tension that must be addressed more directly before the campus can be truly diverse.

B-

The College Prowler® Grade on

Diversity: B-

A high grade in Diversity indicates that ethnic minorities and international students have a notable presence on campus and that students of different economic backgrounds, religious beliefs, and sexual preferences are well-represented.

Guys & Girls

The Lowdown On...
Guys & Girls

Male Undergrads:
47%

Female Undergrads:
53%

Birth Control Available?

Yes, at Searle Health Services

Dress Code

Style is casual across the board at NU. Don't expect any bold fashions here—most stick with the classic Gap look. Plus, in winter, students bundle up in layers—it's not exactly sexy, but at least you won't get frostbite.

Did You Know?

Top Places to Hook Up:

1. Shakespeare Garden
2. Lakefill
3. University Library core
4. Dorm room/apartment
5. North or South Beach

Social Scene

Students at Northwestern are very studious, and while the Greek scene is huge, academics always seem to come first. Career advancement and ambition often override social activities, and many outsiders view NU students as anti-social. However, if the timing is right—during Dead Week, a school break, or a non-taxing time of the quarter—students can come out of their shells and party with the best of them.

Hookups or Relationships?

Students tend to be in it for the long haul, or, just as likely, ready for a fling before stressful finals roll around. This stems from the studious nature of NU students; so many undergraduates are determined to succeed academically, it takes a persistent paramour to catch one's long-term fancy. But, just as hardcore partying is an occasional leisure, getting down and dirty in the short term happens fairly often.

Best Place to Meet Guys/Girls

Evanston's not the most NU-friendly town, and the bars tend to turn into meat markets—particularly 1800 Club and the Keg. It's a lot more common that you'll spark a relationship with someone you share mutual interests with—your fraternity and sorority often pair off, you were partners in Dance Marathon, you worked on the *Daily Northwestern* together. You may be tempted to hook up with that hottie down the hall, but beware, "dormcest" is frowned upon more or less universally, as it often ends badly.

Students Speak Out On...
Guys & Girls

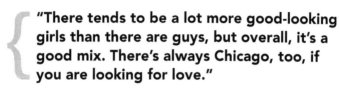

"There tends to be a lot more good-looking girls than there are guys, but overall, it's a good mix. There's always Chicago, too, if you are looking for love."

Q "In my opinion, **most of the guys are nerdy, not hot**. As for the females, I have seen some really hot ones that I would like to get to know better."

Q "The guys are really pretty nice. **There are definitely some hot boys on this campus, but a lot are gay**. The girls are nice. With both sexes, there are definitely all sorts of people here—from ditzes to geeks to really artistic people, it really varies."

Q "I guess this campus is not known for its attractiveness, but there are many very nice, attractive people. You will hear—and I think it's partly true—that **many people on this campus are obsessed with work** and are otherwise pompous and annoying."

Q "I tend to find that most people at Northwestern are either **very attractive or very unattractive**."

Q "Guys are hotter in this freshman class than in my year. Basically, we call guys 'Northwestern cute.' I guess the answer would be no, they're not hot. **Girls are all really in shape**."

Q "We developed the phrase 'Northwestern cute' for the guys. There are some good-looking guys, but **the shortage makes your standards lower**."

Q "In my opinion, there are more good-looking girls than guys, **but many guys would disagree with me**."

Q "I would not describe most of the guys as particularly good looking. There are some, though. **There are a lot of girls who are very into their looks**, but I don't know if that means they are actually good looking."

Q "There are lots of hot girls who will never find a guy at Northwestern. **Dating is pretty rare here; either you're totally single or totally committed**. That's been very frustrating for lots of people I have talked to."

Q "There are probably fewer attractive girls than at a state school, but there are enough. There are plenty of handsome guys like myself here, and many of them are nice. Just like anywhere, **there are different crowds, and you'll find people that are like you**."

Q "The people can be nice, **but you definitely have to seek out different people**. The average Northwestern student in my opinion is a white, upper-middle-class kid from the Midwest, California, Texas, or the Northeast."

Q "Everyone here knows that the guys are nowhere near as hot as the girls. It's just something that is accepted throughout campus. **Guys that come here are lucky**, because we girls tend to lower our standards when it comes to hooking up with guys. For all you girls out there, don't worry—you can also venture out into Chicago and other nearby schools if you're really picky!"

Q "Sure, *Playboy* did a spread on girls of the Big Ten that featured Northwestern. But, **most of the time, we're bundled up in winter clothes** and cursing the lake effect. Chicks, in general, are way hotter than the guys. The nice thing is that once you get past the sometimes geeky exterior, people have a lot of interesting things to say, which makes them all the more attractive."

Q "You have to know where to look, and **it totally depends on your type**. Personally, I think NU has some fairly attractive people."

Q "I don't know, out of 8,000 undergrads, **you're bound to get a broad range from gorgeous to hideous**. I've had a girlfriend from high school since the moment I walked on campus, so I've kept my blinders on."

Q "If you dated a lot in high school, don't think it's going to be the same at college, because it probably won't. There are a lot of great, attractive, well-adapted guys out there, but they are definitely outnumbered by the dorky guys who have no dating experience and are socially inept. For some reason, there seems to be **a negative correlation between intelligence and level of social development**."

Q "For a top-tier school, Northwestern students tend to be well rounded and relatively normal, but in comparison to state schools and high school, there are a lot more students here who have not taken the time to develop their social skills adequately. **That doesn't mean that they are not attractive or date-worthy**, it just means they don't have the experience you might normally expect of college students."

Q "Between October and May, I tend to forget that attractive girls exist here, but **as soon as the weather turns nice, they emerge**."

Q "Most of the people seem very friendly and respectful on campus. I definitely think there are plenty of hot girls on campus. The only problem is that the **girls are too busy to date or too picky**."

Q "**South Campus guys are either scrawny or gay**. Go north. Most girls are really pretty, though. I don't understand why this is."

Q "The dating scene is sucky, but that doesn't mean it's non-existent. **Many people are too busy for relationships**, but it leaves a large space for fun hookups! I don't recommend dating someone in your dorm because it can get messy, but other than that, college is a time to experiment and have fun, which Northwestern students are prone to doing."

The College Prowler Take On...
Guys & Girls

Dating still mystifies much of the Northwestern population. Almost all agree that the girls are more attractive than the men, on the whole, and some wonder whether this kills the dating scene. Students either seem to be in committed relationships headed toward marriage, or having one fling after another with the acceptable members of the opposite sex who reside somewhere on campus. Ambition for academics often puts a damper on sizzling passion, which can be frustrating when looking for a date to the formal.

If you dig a little deeper than first impressions, the student body of Northwestern is very dateable. However, cold winter weather often puts a damper on students looking to get down—who wants to make out when three layers of parkas separates you? Look closely at your prospects, and don't discount someone if they're initially a little uptight. NU kids are known for being socially inept, but most are interesting and driven. If you're looking for wild fun, Northwestern may not be your cup of tea, but if you can see the value of that hottie in Associated Student Government, you may be quite happy with the meet-and-greet scene.

The College Prowler® Grade on
Guys: C

A high grade for Guys indicates that the male population on campus is attractive, smart, friendly, and engaging, and that the school has a decent ratio of guys to girls.

The College Prowler® Grade on
Girls: B

A high grade for Girls not only implies that the women on campus are attractive, smart, friendly, and engaging, but also that there is a fair ratio of girls to guys.

Athletics

The Lowdown On...
Athletics

Athletic Division:
NCAA Division I

Conference:
Big Ten

School Mascot:
Wildcat

Men Playing Varsity Sports:
220 (6%)

Women Playing Varsity Sports:
208 (5%)

➔

Men's Varsity Sports:

Baseball
Basketball
Football
Golf
Soccer
Swimming
Tennis
Wrestling

Women's Varsity Sports:

Basketball
Cross country
Fencing
Field hockey
Golf
Lacrosse
Soccer
Softball
Swimming
Tennis
Volleyball

Intramurals:

Basketball
Dodgeball
Flag football
Floor hockey
Soccer
Softball
Tennis
Ultimate Frisbee
Volleyball
Wallyball

Club Sports:

Aikido
Baseball
Basketball
Crew
Cricket
Cycling
Equestrian
Fencing
Gymnastics
Ice hockey
Jujitsu
Karate
Lacrosse
Roller hockey
Rugby
Running
Sailing
Ski racing
Soccer
Squash
Tae kwon do
Tennis
Ultimate Frisbee
Volleyball
Water polo

Getting Tickets

Tickets are easy to get and cheap for students—if your parents come into town, it may be a little more expensive. But unless Northwestern turns into a "real" Big Ten school anytime soon, you can count on cheap, uncrowded sports action. Get tickets at Ryan Field or by calling (847) 491-CATS.

Most Popular Sports

Football and basketball command the most respect and bring in the biggest audiences. But just remember, we're a top 10 school for academics, so it's not too big of a deal if our teams do not always finish in the top 25.

Most Overlooked Teams

Most women's teams fade into the background, although they are among the strongest at the school. Take women's tennis—the team sends someone to the NCAA women's tennis quarterfinals every year. And our fencing team—they're regularly ranked among the top five in the nation.

Athletic Fields

Blomquist Recreation Center

The primary workout facility for South Campus, the BQ attracts mostly women—most sporting Greek letters. There isn't much equipment here, though it was recently expanded. Still, plan on some long waits while some snooty chick blasts her buns on the elliptical.

Henry Crown Sports Pavilion and the Dellora A. and Lester J. Norris Aquatic Center

Affectionately termed SPAC, this facility boasts racquetball courts, hundreds of exercise machines, an indoor track, and a pool. There are also basketball and tennis courts, so virtually any sport you could imagine is at your fingertips. You may have to compete with one of your professors or an Evanston resident for the treadmill, but this is your best bet for workout digs on campus.

(Athletic Fields, continued)

Drysdale Field

Another hub for varsity athletics, you can catch the up-and-coming women's softball team. No matter who you are, you gotta love the diamond girls.

Floyd Long Field

Up north and away from the lake, this is the perfect spot for a competitive match—be it soccer, football, rugby, or lacrosse.

Lakeside Field

Catch a glimpse of women's lacrosse action or take in one of the other, less-talked-about sports at Lakeside Field. If on the off chance it's empty, feel free to kick around a ball or rope your ragtag friends into a game of tackle football, no holds barred.

McGaw Memorial Arena

Home to NU's basketball team, McGaw is a spacious stadium with tons of leg room. In addition to hosting basketball in the winter, McGaw also acts as the largest indoor space at Northwestern—you'll be herded into the bleachers for an inaugural address by the University president, and your school's graduation may be held here.

Patten Gymnasium

Closely located to the frat quad, Patten is a training facility equipped with basketball courts and free weights. Most of the people up here are serious athletes, so don't be surprised to see varsity men and women working up a sweat.

Rocky Miller Park

NU's baseball field is host to high-speed action, so grab a hotdog and enjoy the show during spring quarter.

Ryan Field

This recently-renovated football arena is equipped with new seating, posh extras, and real grass—rather than artificial turf. However, even these amenities have yet to attract huge crowds, as most games do not sell out. However, you likely will spend a few Saturdays every fall up here, so thank your lucky stars for the ample seating in the student section.

Students Speak Out On...
Athletics

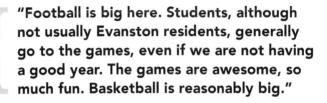

{ **"Football is big here. Students, although not usually Evanston residents, generally go to the games, even if we are not having a good year. The games are awesome, so much fun. Basketball is reasonably big."**

Q "Varsity sports are pretty big, as are club sports and intramurals. Being a Big Ten school, **we have a pretty big conference to compete in**. We don't always do well, but we certainly try."

Q "The campus empties for football and basketball games. **Everyone is there with purple faces and waving pom-poms**. They are good times. I play a club sport— softball—which is more like high school varsity sports than college. Participating in a college sport is pretty crazy. However, if you're really good and love practicing, by all means, participate."

Q "**There is opportunity to join IM teams all year round**, and you don't need to be part of a formal campus organization (like a fraternity) to form a team and join a league."

Q "Our football team has performed well as of late. Our basketball team blows, though. **I have no hope for them**. A lot of our women's sports are regularly ranked year after year. IM sports are huge."

Q "**I have tons of friends who participate in IM sports**. SPAC, our athletic center, was remodeled just a few years ago, and it is awesome. It has everything you would want in an athletic center and more."

Q "**Football is huge and everyone goes to games**. IM sports and club sports are also very easy to get involved in."

Q "Varsity sports aren't a huge deal, except for football because it's Big Ten! **The games are amazing**! A lot of people play IM sports and really enjoy that."

Q "I don't know much about varsity sports other than football. **Lots of people go to football games, but that's about it**. Basketball isn't big. IM leagues seem to have good participation, but I don't really know since I don't play in one."

Q "**Our varsity sports here suck**, so not too many people go, but football and basketball games are a ton of fun. Our basketball team is getting better."

Q "IM sports depend on the dorm you are in to a certain degree, but in general, **a lot of people play**."

Q "There are plenty of both IM and varsity sports, but as usual, **football and basketball gets the most attention**. I am actively involved in club water polo here at NU."

Q "I guess there's a medium amount of support for varsity sports. None of the spectator sports are very good, so I'm sure that makes a difference. **IM sports normally seem pretty popular**."

Q "There are a lot of sports to get involved in. I'm not really interested, so that's a pretty big blank for me. **If you want to get involved, you have lots of opportunity** as far as I can tell. If you don't, you'll forget that sports even exist."

Q "**Watching varsity sports is depressing**. **Following them closely is even more depressing**. NU is in a conference where the teams are pitted against athletes recruited and nursed through school. For the most part, athletes are here because of talent, as well as academics. There are really high graduation rates for players, but this commitment to academia comes back to bite us in the Big Ten, full of schools with large undergraduate bases and less stringent standards."

Q "Varsity sports are pretty big, but **nothing in comparison to other Big Ten schools**. It's very possible to live on campus and have no idea what's going on with the football team, but at the same time, you can go to games and really get into the whole college sports atmosphere."

Q "**Football is popular, other sports less so**. IM sports are pretty popular, especially softball."

Q "Football seems to be the biggest varsity sport. Most athletes live on North Campus. **Students from all over campus and all disciplines participate in IM sports**."

Q "The football games are really fun if you go with a big group and get into the cheering and action of the game. Quite a few students go for such a smart school. **Intramural sports are pretty big**—most dorms and Greek groups have teams, and they have the standards, I think—like football, soccer, softball, Frisbee to name a few."

Q "Club sports seem pretty cool—all the benefits of exercise without necessarily the commitment for varsity. **Rugby and sailing have parties that are amazing**—always fun, always out of control."

The College Prowler Take On...
Athletics

Although NU's football squad is up-and-coming, and even cracked the top 25 for a while in 2005, they still have a long way to go before they garner respect the likes of Michigan or Ohio State—two Big Ten rivals. Most students go to games for the camaraderie, and nothing more. IM and club sports are both fairly popular, but there are also many NU students who quiver at the thought of picking up a pigskin or a baseball bat.

NU is not an athletic powerhouse—and probably never will be. We're more proud of our academic achievements anyhow. Half the appeal of football games is socializing. After a few pre-game beers, it's off to Ryan Field where maybe our team will upset a perennial powerhouse and prove to the world, once and for all, that the pen is, in fact, mightier than the sword.

The College Prowler® Grade on
Athletics: B

A high grade in Athletics indicates that students have school spirit, that sports programs are respected, that games are well-attended, and that intramurals are a prominent part of student life.

Nightlife

The Lowdown On...
Nightlife

Club and Bar Prowler:
Popular Nightlife Spots!

Club Crawler:

Clubs in Evanston proper are virtually non-existent—most students head to one of the hundreds in Chicago.

Bar Prowler:

Evanston has only allowed liquor on its premises for the last 30 or so years, so it's no wonder the bar scene is relatively small and unimpressive. There are also laws that mandate Evanston bars must do 50 percent of their business in food and 50 percent in liquor. Still, if you're looking for a night out, but are too tired to head down to Chicago, hit these old favorites.

1800 Club

1800 Sherman Ave.

(847) 733-7900

Famous for being "the spot" to pick up sorority girls in tight black pants. Quickly turns into a meat market, so if you have self respect, watch how you act.

Bar Louie

1520 Sherman Ave.

(847) 733-8300

www.barlouieamerica.com

A fairly typical restaurant and bar chain, but less populated by fraternity and sorority members than other local bars.

The Keg

810 Grove St.

(847) 869-9987

The food is sketchy, but nonetheless students flock, mostly on Monday and Thursday nights. Fridays here can be a little quiet, so prowl around for action elsewhere.

Las Palmas

817 University Pl.

(847) 328-2555

On Friday and Saturday nights, this place is filled with (often underage) students drinking overpriced margaritas and enjoying themselves.

Mark II Lounge (the Deuce)

7436 N. Western Ave., Chicago

(Mark II, continued)

(773) 465-9675

An institution, if only because it stays open until 4 a.m. and offers sports on TV and pool tables aplenty. It's not high class, but if a drink you're looking for, a drink you will find here.

Pete Miller's Seafood and Prime Steak

1557 Sherman Ave.

(847) 328-0399

Cool spot with great steaks. A little more suitable for a drink and a date than some of the other bars around town, and free jazz—a terrific combination.

Prairie Moon

1502 Sherman Ave.

(847) 864-0328

www.prairiemoonrestaurant.com

Good food and excellent drinks, this new establishment has been raking in customers. It's a lot more low-key than other bars, so expect the more crunchy, artistic types to patronize this place.

Tommy Nevin's Pub

1450 Sherman Ave.

(847) 869-0450

www.tommynevins.com

English and Irish taps, so beer drinkers' interests are always piqued. This hip night spot was recently renovated and serves up delicious meals as well as hot music acts.

Student Favorites:

1800 Club

The Keg

Mark II Lounge (the Deuce)

Las Palmas

Prairie Moon

Tommy Nevin's Pub

Favorite Drinking Games:

Beer Pong

Card Games (A$$hole)

Century Club

Quarters

Power Hour

Bars Close At:

2 a.m.

Useful Resources for Nightlife:

www.metromix.com

Organization Parties

Most clubs, sports, or activities you join will sponsor their own parties. Some are private, some are open to everyone at the University—these may charge a cover. School-sponsored parties, such as those thrown by academic departments, are usually more conservative affairs—though they often have luscious food.

Frats

See the Greek section!

Students Speak Out On...
Nightlife

"Some big names are: the Keg, the Deuce, Prairie Moon, and 1800 Club. They are all 21-and-over, but if you have a mediocre ID, you are fine. Thursdays are big nights to go out. Also, we are close to Chicago, so you have those bars and clubs, too."

Q "**Bars and clubs in Evanston are virtually non-existent**. Most of the partying centers on the Greek scene, though Greeks don't dominate. Bars and clubs in Chicago are virtually endless."

Q "As far as Evanston goes, there is always the Keg. The Keg is a bar about two blocks from campus—it's always packed with students, especially on Thursday nights. **They are easier on IDs than ... well, anywhere**. **You can use a note from your mom to get in**. Not really, but almost. It's legendary."

Q "The city of Evanston is also working to extend the hours that bars can serve alcohol, which helps. But then **there is always Chicago, which is about a 10-minute drive to the border**, where there is another infamous bar, the Deuce. Everyone goes to the deuce after the Keg because it's open until 4 a.m., as Chicago has more lenient liquor license laws."

Q "There are plenty of parties and people who like to get drunk if that's your scene, though. The Greek system makes sure of that. As for bars and clubs, there are really only a few—1800 Club, Bar Louie, and maybe one or two others. **If you want to go to a real club you'll probably have to take a trip downtown**!"

Q "With a declining on-campus party scene, the bars and clubs have become more significant. There are four or five really nice ones right around campus: the Keg, 1800 Club, Bar Louie, Prairie Moon, and Nevin's. On Monday and Thursday nights, students like to spend the later part of the night, from 1 a.m. to 4 a.m. at this bar called the Mark II or 'The Deuce,' which is located about a 10-minute cab ride away in North Chicago. However, the Deuce's popularity is rooted in the fact that bars in Evanston are forced to close at 1 a.m. But this is changing, and **soon, most bars in Evanston will close at 3 a.m. on weekends**."

Q "Northwestern only has two real campus bars, 1800 Club and The Keg, **which are pretty much where the underclassmen go with their fakes**. Most people who are of age go to the bars in the city down by Loyola, Wrigleyville, or downtown."

Q "I haven't enjoyed a lot of the parties I've gone to, but that's probably because I don't know most of the people there—if I did I imagine it would be a lot more fun. I guess parties are about what you would expect: **loud, alcohol, sometimes dancing, crowded**."

Q "For great parties on campus, check out the Rainbow Alliance. **Even if you're not gay, these parties rock**. I'm straight and I go to every single party because it's amazing. I've met some amazing people there. As far as clubs, if you're not 21, forget about it!"

Q "Some parties are okay. Sometimes, the **people tend to stick with the group they came with** instead of mingling. Pete Miller's is a great place for live music and a restaurant. A lot of students tend to like Las Palmas or Nevin's."

Q "There really isn't a lot of partying in dorms, but if you have friends out of the housing system, you're cool. **Hot, sweaty apartment parties** are usually the place to be on a Friday night if you're underage. 1800 Club, The Keg and other bars are kind of a meat market, and if you have any self respect, you avoid them. Theme parties are big, and whether you're looking for a Polka Party or a throwback to the 1980s, there's usually someone, somewhere who can help you out."

The College Prowler Take On...
Nightlife

There aren't many options in Evanston, but we take what we can get. Nevin's Live is gaining in popularity, and 1800 Club, the Keg, and the Deuce are all dependable, if not exciting. Most people with discriminating taste (and who are of legal age) will head to Chicago if they're interested in partaking in nightlife.

There isn't much you can say when you go to college in a town considered the birthplace of the Prohibition movement. Thank your lucky stars you're young, because your parents didn't have the opportunity to hit town close to home—even if it is just Pete Miller's on a Monday night. Although the club and bar scene in NU territory is pathetic, a short cab ride to Chicago opens up a world of dancing, dating, and ice-cold frosty brews.

The College Prowler® Grade on

Nightlife: C+

A high grade in Nightlife indicates that there are many bars and clubs in the area that are easily accessible and affordable. Other determining factors include the number of options for the under-21 crowd and the prevalence of house parties.

Greek Life

The Lowdown On...
Greek Life

Number of Fraternities: 24	**Undergrad Men in Fraternities:** 32%
Number of Sororities: 19	**Undergrad Women in Sororities:** 38%

Fraternities:

Alpha Epsilon Pi
Alpha Phi Alpha Fraternity, Inc.
Beta Theta Pi
Chi Phi
Chi Psi
Delta Chi
Delta Tau Delta
Delta Upsilon
Evans Scholars
Kappa Alpha Psi Fraternity Inc.
Lambda Chi Alpha
Lambda Phi Epsilon
Omega Delta Phi
Phi Beta Sigma Fraternity Inc.
Phi Delta Theta
Phi Gamma Delta (FIJI)
Phi Kappa Psi
Pi Kappa Alpha
Sigma Alpha Epsilon
Sigma Chi
Sigma Nu
Sigma Phi Epsilon
Theta Chi
Zeta Beta Tau

Multicultural Colonies:

National Pan-Hellenic Council and the Multicultural Greek Council boast a small but strong presence, with several colonies of historically black, Asian, and Hispanic fraternities and sororities.

Sororities:

Alpha Chi Omega
Alpha Delta Pi
Alpha Kappa Alpha Sorority, Inc.
Alpha Phi
Chi Omega
Delta Delta Delta
Delta Gamma
Delta Sigma Theta Sorority, Inc.
Delta Zeta
Gamma Phi Beta
Kappa Alpha Theta
Kappa Delta
Kappa Kappa Gamma
Kappa Phi Lambda
Lambda Theta Alpha Latin Sorority, Inc.
Pi Beta Phi
Sigma Gamma Rho Sorority, Inc.
Sigma Lambda Gamma
Zeta Phi Beta Sorority, Inc.

Other Greek Organizations:

Gamma Sigma Alpha
Interfraternity Council
Order of Omega
Panhellenic Association
Rho Lambda

Students Speak Out On...
Greek Life

{

"The Greek scene is pretty big here, but it's not out of control like it is at some state schools. Our Greek system is also a lot different; people who you wouldn't expect to find in houses are."

Q "Greek life does not dominate the social scene. While people 'go Greek,' many leave during their time here, and it is more than possible to find a good group of friends to enjoy college with outside of the Greek community. I think, in some respects, **going Greek makes it harder to enjoy your free time**, because there are always obligations."

Q "Greek life is pretty big, but not as big as it is on some state school campuses. I was affiliated with a house my freshman year, but then **I decided it wasn't for me**. I didn't experience any less of a social life because of it."

Q "**They don't really dominate**. I enjoy being Greek, but once you meet people, they do not treat you different if you aren't Greek."

Q "There are 14 sorority houses in the Panhel (Pan-Hellenic) system. Most people seem to rush, but in actuality, only about 35 percent of the campus is Greek. **I would say it dominates a lot of the social scene**. I am in a house, but I have a lot of friends who are not."

Q "Approximately 30 percent of the students go Greek. This may seem high, but I have found that **it doesn't really separate the student body all that much**."

Q "Greek life dominates the social scene, but **you don't have to be Greek to have a good time**. You rush at the beginning of winter quarter, which is better than fall rush because it gives you the chance to meet people outside of Greek life."

Q "**I am not in a sorority, and it has never been a problem for me**. You can still find plenty to do. However, a lot of girls are in them. My boyfriend is in a frat, and he has been happy with it."

Q "I'm in a sorority and love it. It gives you the chance to get close with a good group of girls and have nice social events and stuff. **The food rocks in the sororities**. But, my really close friends aren't in sororities, and it is no big deal. I would say that it is a bigger deal, socially, for guys to be in frats because the party scene revolves around the frats."

Q "Yes, Greek life is big here. **I am not in a sorority, though, and I'm still having fun**! I will say that it definitely helps your social life to be in a sorority, but it all depends on the kinds of fun you want to have."

Q "About a third of students are in frats and sororities, and they do make up most of the parties and many events on campus. But I'm not involved with a frat at all, and I have a good time, so **it's not at all necessary**. There are plenty of things to do in the city if you're bored on campus, too."

Q "Greek life is highly visible—**it's certainly possible to live in an all-Greek world**, I think, but that doesn't at all mean that there isn't enough other stuff to do on campus."

Q "You hear about it a lot, but an outsider will probably not feel particularly overwhelmed by the Greek system. I think 40 percent of the student body is Greek. **So you can pretty much take it or leave it**."

Q "**I'm not in a sorority, so it's hard for me to say**. My friends in Greek houses enjoy it and they have lots of cool events, but I wouldn't say Greek life dominates the social scene—at least not on South Campus."

Q "I'm in the 'alternative' Greek scene (a non-IFC fraternity). **I find that it's a big part of my social life**, but it doesn't prevent me from doing other things."

Q "There are still plenty of things to do without being a sorority/fraternity. It doesn't dominate the social scene and is really expensive to be part of one. It depends what kind of person you are. If you are having trouble making friends or don't really partake in many outside activities, joining a sorority or fraternity would probably be a great thing to do because **it will give you an instant group of friends**. However, it will also wipe clean your bank account."

Q "It depends. **If you live in a residential college freshman year, you're probably going to build your social scene that way**, especially for the first year or two. After that, it's by interests, campus groups, and Greek organizations, I imagine."

Q "You can definitely categorize what house people are in by how they look—**I've never met a Theta who isn't blonde**. However, most of the sorority girls and some of the frat guys are down-to-earth and intellectual, though they may have a proclivity to party a bit more."

The College Prowler Take On...
Greek Life

It's a Greek world, and the rest of us are just living in it. About 35 percent of all students at Nu are in some Greek house, but the consoling part is that NU doesn't necessarily have all the trappings of a traditional Greek system. There are fraternities and sororities known for partying, but there are also houses where the emphasis is on community and togetherness, not cattiness and testosterone.

Going Greek is a very personal choice. A lot of people you wouldn't expect to go Greek will join a house, and others that you peg as partiers won't. Some outsiders to the community quibble that it's akin to buying your friends, but tensions between Greeks and non-Greeks are not an issue here. More likely than not, even if you choose to forgo rushing, you'll have access to fraternity and sorority events—and all the parties you so desire to attend.

The College Prowler® Grade on

Greek Life: A-

A high grade in Greek Life indicates that sororities and fraternities are not only present, but also active on campus. Other determining factors include the variety of houses available and the respect the Greek community receives from the rest of the campus.

Drug Scene

The Lowdown On...
Drug Scene

Most Prevalent Drugs on Campus:
Alcohol
Marijuana
Mushrooms

Alcohol-Related Referrals:
366

Alcohol-Related Arrests:
4

Drug-Related Referrals:
14

Drug-Related Arrests:
28

Drug Counseling Programs:
Alcoholics Anonymous
Counseling and Psychological Services

Students Speak Out On...
Drug Scene

"They're here. I mean, pot is pretty much everywhere, but there aren't too many people who do the hard stuff. There definitely are people who do, but it's not as pronounced as at a lot of other colleges."

Q "I don't know too much about the drug scene. **I know that alcohol is certainly the most used substance**. It's in ample supply, but I don't hear or see much involving other drugs."

Q "The drug scene is not very easy to break into at first, but drugs are definitely around campus. Most people just smoke weed, but '**shrooms, coke, and X (ecstasy) are around every once in a while**, too."

Q "**Drugs don't seem to be a big problem**, but alcohol is always a battle for the administration."

Q "Drugs will be there if you want them, and if you don't, then **you'll never see them**."

Q "**Drinking is big**. There definitely are drugs, but if you're not into it, you probably won't see them too often. I think it varies by social circle. There is definitely lots of pot, but I haven't physically seen anything else, although it does go on, though."

Q "It's **virtually non-existent**. A minority of students smoke pot on occasion."

Q "From what I can say, if you are into that sort of thing, you can pretty much find whatever you want. If not, **you can also completely avoid it altogether**."

Q "**If you want to find people who use drugs, you can**. If you don't, you can avoid them. I haven't seen anybody using drugs, but it happens a lot."

Q "In my experience, **there are some drugs floating around campus**; it's mainly your decision whether or not to get involved. There definitely will not be any pressure to participate if you want to avoid the drug scene."

Q "There are probably all manner of drugs being done at Northwestern, but to what extent, I'm not sure. Marijuana is the most popular by far, though, at least among people I know. If you want an environment where there are no drugs or where you won't feel pressured about doing drugs, **that's not too hard to find**."

Q "**Dude, where's my pot brownie**? You can usually do drugs without getting caught. Not many people do much more than pot, and it's minimal at that—a toke with a friend at a huge party. I've ran into a couple people who do 'shrooms or trip occasionally, but many bookish students would be shocked."

Q "It fluctuates. Depends where you are. **You'll always find that one guy that does every drug on the planet**, but for the most part, people don't do anything."

Q "Alcohol is much more prevalent than any illegal drugs, though. Except maybe for pot. It's hard to tell. **There are a lot of sober people**, however, and you're not going to find anyone forcing drugs on you."

Q "My impression is that **most people drink and a majority of students smoke pot**, but harder drug users are in the minority. It really runs the spectrum, though."

Q "By far, the most popular drug on campus (after alcohol) is marijuana. **I think most people, even if they don't use, tolerate it**, and don't look down on others who do. There are a lot of people who are 'occasional' users at parties and such. Beyond that, most other drugs are available on campus, and they are used regularly. The important thing to remember is that drug use is not isolated to outsiders or a 'drug culture.' Rather, it's just another part of life, along with sex, drinking, and partying."

Q "There aren't many people that do a lot of hardcore drugs on campus. There is a bunch of pot smoking, but no one feels pressure to indulge unless they choose to based on free will. **It's there if you want it, but it's not something that can't be avoided**."

The College Prowler Take On...
Drug Scene

Northwestern students? Risking academics or an internship just to smoke a joint? As with any college campus, if you want marijuana, you can find it, but most likely, you'll discover stockpiles of Smirnoff and Bacardi—perfectly legal, thank you very much. A lot of people partake solely in social situations, a nip of vodka at a mixer, or a toke off a communal joint at an off-campus house party.

There are exceptions to every rule, and everyone knows that one guy who reeks of pot every time he leaves his room. So, if you want to partake, that's your business. But if not, there won't be any pressure, and it's entirely possible that you'll spend four years at Northwestern without ever coming down with a serious case of the munchies.

B

The College Prowler® Grade on

Drug Scene: B

A high grade in the Drug Scene indicates that drugs are not a noticeable part of campus life; drug use is not visible, and no pressure to use them seems to exist.

Campus
Strictness

The Lowdown On...
Campus Strictness

What Are You Most Likely to Get Caught Doing on Campus?
- Public drunkenness
- Public nudity
- Underage drinking

Students Speak Out On...
Campus Strictness

{ **"I do my fair share of everything, and I have never had a problem with police. I'd say they're right in the middle of the strictness scale. You'll have no problem drinking in your room with some friends if you're smart about it."**

Q "They watch pretty well. **One person got busted for a meth lab on campus in his dorm**. They really aren't too bad. However, it's not like we're a state school where anything goes. If a cop sees you drinking, they will most likely just tell you to throw it away. As far as parties go, cops come three times. The first time they warn you, the second time they start telling people to leave, and the third time they fine you. It's pretty lenient."

Q "Generally, **parties in the dorms don't get broken up as long as people are quiet**. I think with weed the RAs tend to be stricter; if they smell it, they will call the cops. Those kinds of violations are generally handled in-house and are not referred to Evanston police. Thus, they don't carry the kind of punishments that someone in the 'real world' might receive."

Q "**The police always look the other way when it comes to drinking and drugs**. All they do is refer students to the student affairs office, and the University usually deals with the problem internally through counseling services."

Q "The campus police are cool about drinking. If they catch you drinking **at an off-campus party, they just tell you to leave**. The University is strict about drinking in the dorms, but if you're smart about it, you can get away with it."

Q "As far as drinking is concerned, the police are very tolerable. **They are much stricter about drugs**. But if a party is broken up and there is underage drinking, the cops generally do not have a problem except with the people who are hosting the party."

Q "Campus police aren't really the ones who would bust you, more likely an RA in a dorm or the Evanston Police at an apartment. **I don't hear about a lot of people getting arrested or anything**, and a cop was very nice to us once. In terms of RAs, it depends who you have."

Q "They're pretty lenient, unless there's a huge raging out-of-control party. But just hope that if you get caught, it's by your RA, cause **otherwise, you have to pay a big fine and it goes on your record**."

Q "They're pretty strict, but **on their best day, I doubt they'd catch 5 percent** of the people committing offenses."

Q "Most people do drugs and drink underage without ever getting caught. **If you are stupid about it, then the police will take action**."

Q "They are usually pretty understanding when dealing with parties. **They don't go out of their way to bust students**. They'll usually just ask everyone to leave. If you're smart and don't do anything blatant, you're fine."

Q "They break up parties when people are drinking and I'm sure they would stop people from doing drugs if they caught them. **Campus police really seem to be more focused on keeping the campus safe** as opposed to enforcing the drinking age."

Q "I'd say they're kind of strict at times, but there are ways around them. In general, **if you don't drink in public and don't make a jerk of yourself, there'll be no problem**. Most of the regulations, however, are due to University liability—a lot of universities are being forced to crack down due to lawsuits. We are a dry campus (meaning there are consequences if caught), but there has been a push for allowing wet fraternities and a bar in Norris."

The College Prowler Take On...
Campus Strictness

We may have our own police force, but Northwestern's finest are more concerned about protecting the University, than about sniffing out every underage drinker. Drinking in public or traipsing around like an idiot will get you caught, but if you're hosting a small get-together with your guest-list comprised of mostly civilized human beings, you're most likely in the clear.

That said, don't be stupid. If students abuse this laxity, we'll no longer be able to quietly enjoy ourselves and the occasional drunken beer fest. Play by their rules, bend them a little—but don't stomp all over them. And if you get the chance to let loose, for God's sake take it—the party scene at NU could use a little livening up.

The College Prowler® Grade on

Campus
Strictness: B+

A high Campus Strictness grade implies an overall lenient atmosphere; police and RAs are fairly tolerant, and the administration's rules are flexible.

Parking

The Lowdown On...
Parking

Approximate Parking Permit Cost:

$426 annually. Cost decreases by $35 monthly after October.

Parking Services:

Campus Police & Parking Regulation

1819 Hinman Ave.

(847) 491-3319

www.northwestern.edu/up/ parking/index.html

Freshmen Allowed to Park?

No

Parking Permits:

To get a permit, you must be a senior or grad student.

Did You Know?

Best Places to Find a Parking Spot:

By the lake or sailing center, in the large lot—and it's still hit or miss.

Good Luck Getting a Parking Spot Here!

Virtually anywhere on campus. Parking is tight, and parking enforcement officials are not shy about ticketing cars.

Students Speak Out On...
Parking

"Parking is awful. Unless you live far off campus, you can't park on campus during the week until you are a senior."

Q "Parking is non-existent. Freshmen, sophomores, and most juniors aren't allowed cars on campus, but if you really have to have a car, there are garages that will charge you monthly to park there. I know some freshmen that have done that, and it's not too bad. Considering that everything in Evanston worth seeing is really in walking distance, and that in order to get into the city all you need to do is walk about a block to the El train, **having a car is not crucial**."

Q "**Parking is okay**. I don't have a car, but I think people usually find ample parking available on and off campus."

Q "Parking is horrible in Evanston, just as it is in every other major city or every other suburb close to a city. Northwestern has a lot of parking, but it is usually **limited for seniors, juniors, and faculty**. I didn't bring my car up at all, and I have made it around just as well."

Q "Parking can be a problem if you don't have a permit, and **freshmen aren't issued parking permits**."

Q "**Parking is nearly impossible**. Permits are only for seniors and cost about $300. It's completely ridiculous. There is some street parking, but that is difficult to find, too. Having a car has been quite a hassle for me."

Q "**Evanston has more cars and fewer spaces all the time**. If you're planning on bringing a car, ask yourself if it's worth the expensive permits and the trouble."

Q "It's very hard to park, but most people don't bring cars until junior year at the earliest. You can't get 'official' parking until senior year, though. You end up moving your car around a lot and running from the Evanston parking enforcement cars. **The good news is you don't need a car here**. Public transportation is awesome, and almost everybody takes that. And you walk a lot in Evanston."

Q "**Parking is the devil**."

Q "Parking on campus is near to impossible for students on campus. Most people with cars park on the street, but street parking is really tight, too. I personally chose not to bring a car to school because **I don't think it's worth the hassle**."

Q "Parking on campus is pretty good for the most part. Sometimes, you'll have to walk a little to get to your car, but **you will be able to get a spot**."

Q "**Ha! Parking is nearly impossible**. You can't get a permit until you have senior status (by credits, not years of college) to park on campus and, even then, it's ridiculously expensive. Off campus, there is very little available, but it is somewhat possible if you figure out when they clean which streets."

The College Prowler Take On...
Parking

Parking is a mess, no matter how you slice it. Only seniors can "officially" park on campus. Underclassmen usually resort to parallel parking on Evanston's side streets and alleys. Regardless of age or status, you are likely to accumulate a good number of parking tickets, which most NU students just ignore.

Don't bring a car to NU unless it is absolutely necessary. With a strong public transit system linking the school to Evanston and Chicago, NU doesn't have much of a need for wheels. It's nice to have the option, but it's just another expense—and when you go to a $30,000 a year school, is it really worth it?

The College Prowler® Grade on

Parking: D-

A high grade in this section indicates that parking is both available and affordable, and that parking enforcement isn't overly severe.

Transportation

The Lowdown On...
Transportation

Ways to Get Around Town:

On Campus
By foot
Campus shuttle

Public Transportation
Chicago Transit Authority
www.transitchicago.com
Information on bus routes,
El trains, and Metra trains

Taxi Cabs
American Taxi Dispatch, Inc.
(847) 673-1000

Best Taxi Service
(847) 864-2500

Magic Cab, Inc.
(847) 866-6100

Norshore Cab Association
(847) 864-7500

Car Rentals

Budget
Local: (847) 864-6661
National: (800) 527-0700
www.budget.com

Enterprise
Local: (847) 475-0300
National: (800) 736-8222
www.enterprise.com

Hertz
Local: (847) 733-7553
National: (800) 654-3131
www.hertz.com

Ways to Get Out of Town:

Airports

Midway International Airport
5700 S. Cicero Ave., Chicago
(800) 832-6352

O'Hare International Airport
10000 W. O'Hare, Chicago
(773) 894-2940

Airlines Serving Chicago

American Airlines
(800) 433-7300
www.aa.com

Continental
(800) 523-3273
www.continental.com

Delta
(800) 221-1212
www.delta.com

Northwest
(800) 225-2525
www.nwa.com

(Airlines, continued)

Southwest
(800) 435-9792
www.southwest.com

United
(800) 241-6522
www.united.com

US Airways
(800) 428-4322
www.usairways.com

How to Get to the Airport

A cab ride to the airport costs
$25–$40, depending upon taxi
company and airport

Greyhound

630 W. Harrison St., Chicago
(312) 408-5800
www.greyhound.com

Amtrak

225 South Canal St., Chicago
(800) 872-7245
www.amtrak.com

Travel Agents:

Four Corners Travel Ltd.
1603 Orrington Ave.
(847) 869-3366

STA Travel
900 Church St
(847) 475-5070

Students Speak Out On...
Transportation

"Public transportation is so easy. The El stops at several locations about two blocks from many different areas of the campus."

Q "**Public transportation is very convenient**. The El (Chicago's famous elevated train system) is a really easy way to get downtown, to the airport, and so on. The buses aren't bad either, although they're not as easy to manage."

Q "Public transportation is okay. **The El runs from near campus into Chicago**, but there is a fair amount of switching trains at most times. Also, sometime around 1:30 a.m., the train stops running to Evanston, meaning that if you are coming back from Chicago late, you're stuck in a bad North Chicago neighborhood."

Q "It's very convenient. **The purple line of the El runs right by campus at three different stops**, allowing you to get all around Chicago in less than an hour. Buses and cabs are everywhere, too, and the Metra can get you to downtown Chicago in less than a half hour."

Q "The El is the way to get downtown. **The stops are close to campus and it's only $1.75 to ride**. However, there are some sketchy characters on the El, so I wouldn't ride alone at night."

Q "The El runs right onto our campus, so it's pretty convenient. **The El is definitely not as efficient as, say, the subway in New York**. Still, it's not too bad."

Q "Public transportation is great! The train is just minutes away from the dorms, and you can get into Chicago in less than an hour for just $1.75. **I love the El.**"

Q "The El is pretty convenient to campus and has lots of stops, though **the Purple Line doesn't run all night which is unfortunate.**"

Q "Transportation here is great—you're connected to all parts of the city and most suburbs. However, don't get locked into only taking public transportation. If you **invest in a good pair of walking shoes**, you'll see parts of the city that aren't directly off the El lines."

Q "The El is great for getting into Chicago. **The bus system is okay if you want to head for a western suburb,** but few students ever use it. There's also the Metra, which is more expensive than the El but nicer, and it goes up into Wisconsin a little ways."

Q "**In Evanston, I usually just walk everywhere,** but if I want to go to Chicago or to the mall, I take mass transit and it's really convenient."

Q "**Public transportation is very convenient and cheap.** If you take the El downtown, though, you should allow 45 minutes each way."

The College Prowler Take On...
Transportation

Transportation in and around campus is excellent—from the El to the Metra, buses to cabs, everything you need to escape E-town is virtually at your fingertips. $1.75 brings you into the heart of the city or takes you to a number of swanky, fun neighborhoods. Trains also run fairly late into the night, so there's no need to spend $30 to have a crazed Nascar wannabe (taxi driver) escort you home.

With the cost of parking being what it is, it's no small wonder students look toward the inexpensive option of public transportation. You may run into an occasional eccentric on the El but for the most part, trains are cheap, quick, and easy. If only the women at NU were like public transportation . . .

A-

The College Prowler® Grade on

Transportation: A-

A high grade for Transportation indicates that campus buses, public buses, cabs, and rental cars are readily-available and affordable. Other determining factors include proximity to an airport and the necessity of transportation.

Weather

The Lowdown On...
Weather

Average Temperature:		Average Precipitation:	
Fall:	54°F	Fall:	2.50 in./month
Winter:	23°F	Winter:	1.80 in./month
Spring:	48°F	Spring:	3.50 in./month
Summer:	74°F	Summer:	3.80 in./month

Students Speak Out On...
Weather

"It's great, and it sucks. During spring, summer, and fall, Chicago weather is really nice. But in winter, it is brutal as hell. Yet, I have a lot of friends from California and Florida who love the cold weather."

Q "It's a slight bit chilly, but **most of the time, it is very nice and sunny out**."

Q "**The weather, quite honestly, sucks**. However, there are usually only a few weeks or even a few days where it is truly freezing. This past winter was really pretty mild; we didn't get our first snow till January. However, Chicago weather is notoriously unpredictable. Just last week it was about 40 degrees. Today it's about 75 degrees."

Q "I hate the weather here. It is bitterly cold in the winter, with strong winds. It rains all the time in the spring and is brutally hot in the summer. But there are some nice days, which make it okay, I guess. **The weather is certainly not a plus**."

Q "**Here it rains most of the time, but it is okay**. It's really flat, so it's very windy at times."

Q "The weather is awful, especially in the winter. **People talk about having seasonal depression**. Fall and spring quarters are a lot better. Basically, it is windy, cold, and it rains a lot."

Q "**It's cold**! Bring a scarf, hat, mittens, a heavy coat, and many sweaters."

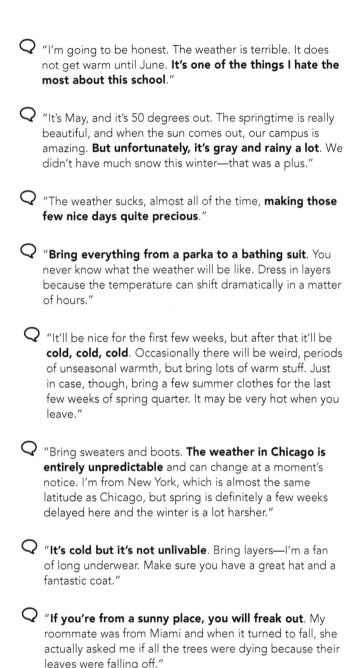

"I'm going to be honest. The weather is terrible. It does not get warm until June. **It's one of the things I hate the most about this school**."

"It's May, and it's 50 degrees out. The springtime is really beautiful, and when the sun comes out, our campus is amazing. **But unfortunately, it's gray and rainy a lot**. We didn't have much snow this winter—that was a plus."

"The weather sucks, almost all of the time, **making those few nice days quite precious**."

"**Bring everything from a parka to a bathing suit**. You never know what the weather will be like. Dress in layers because the temperature can shift dramatically in a matter of hours."

"It'll be nice for the first few weeks, but after that it'll be **cold, cold, cold**. Occasionally there will be weird, periods of unseasonal warmth, but bring lots of warm stuff. Just in case, though, bring a few summer clothes for the last few weeks of spring quarter. It may be very hot when you leave."

"Bring sweaters and boots. **The weather in Chicago is entirely unpredictable** and can change at a moment's notice. I'm from New York, which is almost the same latitude as Chicago, but spring is definitely a few weeks delayed here and the winter is a lot harsher."

"**It's cold but it's not unlivable**. Bring layers—I'm a fan of long underwear. Make sure you have a great hat and a fantastic coat."

"**If you're from a sunny place, you will freak out**. My roommate was from Miami and when it turned to fall, she actually asked me if all the trees were dying because their leaves were falling off."

Q "**The weather is insane**. That's the best way to describe it. Bring everything. Late winter/early spring is the weirdest—it'll go from like 30 degrees one day to 85 the next. It's wild. Also, the wind makes winter rather gross if you don't like bundling up. In addition to a warm hat, get a scarf or little tube-thing for your face (I cover all but my eyes) so you don't get windburn or a frozen face."

Q "One of the awesome things about Chicago is that you never know what to expect from the weather, so bring clothes for all kinds of weather—especially for really hot and really cold. Remember, **Mother Nature isn't a big fan of the weather report around here**."

The College Prowler Take On...
Weather

If Chicago weather had a mental illness, it would be schizophrenia. Where else is it 40 degrees and rainy one day and a blisteringly hot 80 the next? Prepare yourself for the worst, curse Lake Michigan, and resign yourself to wearing layers.

There isn't much you can do about weather, and although most complain about the rapid changes and the biting cold Chicago winters, once you've made it through a year or two, you can survive anything. If you really think that the weather will be that big of a problem, head to one of those pansy schools in the Sun Belt—perhaps Florida Atlantic would be more to your liking?

The College Prowler® Grade on

Weather: D

A high Weather grade designates that temperatures are mild and rarely reach extremes, that the campus tends to be sunny rather than rainy, and that weather is fairly consistent rather than unpredictable.

Report Card Summary

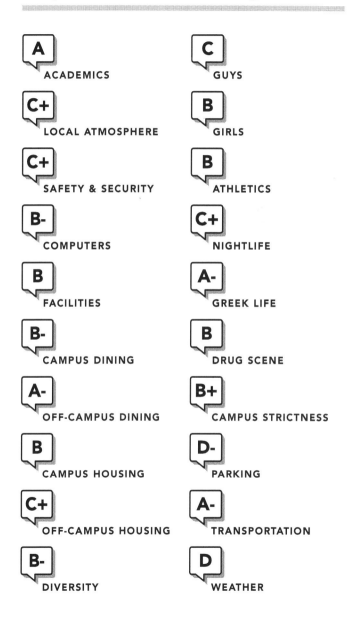

A
ACADEMICS

C+
LOCAL ATMOSPHERE

C+
SAFETY & SECURITY

B-
COMPUTERS

B
FACILITIES

B-
CAMPUS DINING

A-
OFF-CAMPUS DINING

B
CAMPUS HOUSING

C+
OFF-CAMPUS HOUSING

B-
DIVERSITY

C
GUYS

B
GIRLS

B
ATHLETICS

C+
NIGHTLIFE

A-
GREEK LIFE

B
DRUG SCENE

B+
CAMPUS STRICTNESS

D-
PARKING

A-
TRANSPORTATION

D
WEATHER

Overall Experience

Students Speak Out On...
Overall Experience

"I complain a lot, but in all honesty, things here are great. The people are interesting, professors intriguing, and there's never a dull moment. If Evanston sucks, Chicago is a stone's throw away. It's top-of-the-line, and people don't take enough pride in NU's strengths."

"I have enjoyed Northwestern. I don't like all the people, and I think it is unfortunate the partying has decreased and has moved into more expensive bars. **But in general, you will meet great people, learn a lot, and have a lot of fun.**"

Q "I've enjoyed it thus far. It's a tough school, but it's a beautiful campus with great teachers and a great overall environment. I don't think you'd regret coming here, **except for maybe the weather**."

Q "I love Northwestern, and I admit I will miss it when I graduate next month. I am a typical party boy, and I was scared that NU would be a bunch of dorks, but it's really not. **I prefer the liberal, open-minded, intelligent atmosphere at NU**."

Q "It is pretty good. **I'd enjoy it more if there were more things to do in the town**."

Q "It was personally hard for me to adjust to being so far from home. **Now that I'm comfortable, I love it here**. I think there are definitely negatives to NU, and the social scene here leaves much to be desired, but Chicago is awesome. I love what I have gotten involved in at NU."

Q "I do love it here. I made the right decision for me. Sometimes, the party scene sucks, but I really like the people here. At any good school, the classes and professors are going to be similar. I also like the atmosphere. The campus is beautiful and right on Lake Michigan. **I hate the weather, but no college is going to have everything you want**!"

Q "I like it here. If anything, **I'd change the social scene** to include more non-Greek parties and less of a focus on the three bars in this town. The dating thing is frustrating, but not unbearable, and sometimes, you get lucky and find someone awesome. I really like Northwestern. It's got natural beauty going for it, too."

Q "I love NU, and I have never longed to be at another school. There are ups and downs to every institution. **NU has never given me enough downs to make me wish I was elsewhere**."

Q "It's generally good. After freshman year, I was so happy. I felt like I wouldn't rather be anywhere else, and I didn't want to leave for summer. Sophomore year was a bit more realistic—harder, not only because of classes. But **I really do think I'm in the right place**."

Q "**People here can be a little overly intense**, and it can get annoying, but the passion that underlies most people's reason for being here generally makes campus a great place to be."

Q "I love Northwestern, the people, my teachers, the opportunities, and the location. **It's a great place to be if you are a motivated student** who likes to work hard and often succeed."

Q "I think I've grown more as a person here than ever before. **That's at least equally important to what I learn in class**."

Q "I'm really glad I chose Northwestern. I think the environment is such that students can work hard and learn a lot, while still having a social life and getting out into the city frequently. **Administrators have been nothing but helpful** to me, and the teachers are really commendable."

Q "It's not always perfect, but I don't imagine any college is. **Come to Northwestern with a positive attitude, and you can have a great experience**."

Q "My overall experience is that I'm happy with the school, but I don't feel like this is the only place I could be happy. **Sometimes, I wish I could go to school somewhere else just to have another experience**, but I'm not dissatisfied. I think a lot of people's happiness with their school has to do with their personal state of mind and the situation they find themselves in, maybe more than the nature of the school itself."

The College Prowler Take On...
Overall Experience

We bitch, we moan, but there's a reason Northwestern is heralded as one of the best overall undergraduate experiences in America. Academics are stellar, but at the same time, students allow themselves to be students— once that 12-page paper is done, of course. At NU, you will be surprised at how much you learn—and how much of that learning is done outside of the classroom.

Northwestern students don't labor under any illusions that the school is perfect, but despite its shortcomings, most students admit that they wouldn't have had it any other way. Be prepared to be challenged by professors, peers, and your parents when you overcharge their credit cards. But, if you've made the grade, you're obviously able to put forth the extra effort that makes time at NU so worthwhile.

The Inside Scoop

The Lowdown On...
The Inside Scoop

Northwestern Slang:

Know the slang, know the school. Learn the following before coming to Northwestern. The more of these you know, the better off you'll be.

CAESAR – Computer system where you register for classes and keep track of your transcript and financial aid.

CTECs – Course and Teacher Evaluations. Read student ratings of professors before you commit to taking a class with them.

Dormcest – Having an encounter of a sexual nature with someone from your residence hall.

Gone Greek Night – A celebration following rush that results in a good number of drunken hook-ups.

Lakefill – Area of campus bordering Lake Michigan that has bike paths, a fire pit, and fields.

Lagoon – A man-made area filled with water. Watch for ducks and the large fountains that spray all summer long.

➜

North Campus – Generally considered north of Foster-Walker Complex, housing mostly the fraternity quads and engineering students.

Plex – Foster-Walker Complex, a large dorm that features mostly single rooms.

Points – Units on your meal plan that allow you to buy foodstuffs at Norris University Center, Tech Express, Lisa's Café, and University Café.

The Rock – Touchstone of campus that students paint to advertise or philosophize. Guarding the Rock is a ritual everyone must go through.

SAGA – Formerly, the company that ran campus dining—and you'll still run into people who call all the dining halls by this moniker.

Sketch – Something that is shady or questionable; also used as sketchy.

South Campus – South of Foster-Walker Complex; home to the sorority quads and more theater, music, and journalism students.

SPAC – Sports Pavilion and Aquatic Center, the largest workout facility on campus.

Tech – McCormick School of Engineering; refers to students, as well as the large building on North Campus they spend most of their time in.

Things I Wish I Knew Before Coming to Northwestern

• Evanston is a very expensive place to live.

• In-line skates and bikes are useful campus transportation.

• Your home state is not the center of the universe.

Tips to Succeed at Northwestern

• Talk to professors.
• Don't drink too much.
• Get to know fellow students.
• Diversify, but don't get over-involved in activities—college is also for fun, not just networking!

Northwestern Urban Legends

- That NU has the world's third largest building (for its height), the Technological Institute.
- That there is an oppressed, aquatic race living under the Lakefill since it was filled by administrators.
- It is said that if you walk across the seal on Marsh Chapel Plaza, you won't graduate.

School Spirit

- Willie the Wildcat, the mascot, comes in inflatable and traditional guises.
- "Go U Northwestern" is the school's fight song.
- Purple and white are the school's colors.

Traditions

- Painting the Rock
- Gone Greek Night
- Dillo Day: Annual festival of music—and copious amounts of alcohol—that takes place on the Lakefill.
- Dance Marathon
- Dolphin Show
- Waa-Mu Show

Finding a Job or Internship

The Lowdown On...
Finding a Job or Internship

Career Center:

University Career Services
www.northwestern.edu/careers

Advice

Networking is important. Get to know people and they'll help you out in the long run. Professors and advisers are great resources. NU students have high placement rates, so extra effort will get you far in your search.

Services Available:

Career counseling, workshops and searching

Careerline Newsletter

Graduate and Professional School advising

Interview center/on-campus interviews

Job and internship advising and posting access

On-campus job and internship recruiting (MonsterTRAK)

Recruiting assistance for employers

Alumni

The Lowdown On...
Alumni

Alumni Office
1800 Sheridan Rd.
alumni.northwestern.edu

Services Available
Affinity programs
Alumni clubs
Alumni directory
Alumni travel
Continuing education
Northwestern CareerNet
Reunions
Social and athletic programs

Did You Know?

Famous Northwestern Alumni

Rod Blagojevich (Illinois Governor)

Dick Gephardt (Former Missouri U.S. House member)

Charlton Heston (Actor, *The Ten Commandments*, and former NRA President)

Julia Louis-Dreyfuss (Actress, *Seinfeld*)

David Schwimmer (Actor, *Friends*)

Major Alumni Events

See Web site; events are ongoing throughout the year

Alumni Publications

Northwestern Magazine

Student Organizations

This is a sample list of student organizations available at Northwestern. For a more complete list, visit *groups.northwestern.edu.*

Advocacy/Socio-Political

Amnesty International – Northwestern University

College Democrats

College Republicans

Greens

Juice (feminist magazine)

Justice for All (animal rights)

Model United Nations

Objectivist Club

Operation Smile

Peace Project

The Protest (grassroots magazine)

Rainbow Alliance

Students for Environmental and Ecological Development

Students Helping to Organize Awareness of the Holocaust

Women's Coalition

Cultural

Alianza

Asian American Christian Ministry

Black Graduate Student Association

Brown Sugar (Indian a cappella)

CaribNation

Chinese Students and Scholars Association

Circolo Italiano

For Members Only (black students alliance)

Hillel Cultural Life

Japan Club

Jewish Theater Ensemble

Kaibigan (Filipino students alliance)

Korean American Students Association

Muslim-cultural Students Association

Middle Eastern Students Association

National Association of Black Journalists

National Association of Hispanic Journalists

Om (Hindu students council)

Polish-American Students Alliance

Singaporeans and Friends

Thai Club

Turkish Student Association

Entertainment

64 Squares (chess club)

A&O Productions

Arts Alliance Productions

Asterik (all-male a cappella)

Boomshaka

Bridge Club

Catatonics

Dance Marathon

Dead City Productions

(Entertainment, continued)

Flicker Film Festival

Fourtunes Fools (barbershop quartet)

Freshman Fifteen (a cappella)

Graffiti Dancers

Griffin's Tale (children's theater)

Mayfest

Melodious Thunk (a cappella)

Nightcrawlers

Northwestern Class Alliance

Northwestern Student Television

Outing Club

Purple Haze (a cappella)

Significant Others (a cappella)

Ski and Snowboard Club

The Undertones

TONIK Tap

Wave Productions

WildKatz Klezmer Band

Media

AdShop

The Daily Northwestern

Helicon (literary magazine)

Mustardseed

Northwestern Chronicle

Northwestern News Network

Society of Professional Journalists

Syllabus (yearbook)

Religious/Spiritual

Buddhist Study Group

Campus Crusade for Christ

Christians on Campus

Graduate Christian Fellowship

Greek Intervarsity

Harmony in Spirit

InterVarsity Christian Fellowship

Northwestern University Council of Religions

Tuesday Night Fellowship

University Christian Ministry

Service

Alpha Chi Sigma

Alternative Student Breaks

Global Reach

Golden Key International Honor Society

Habitat for Humanity

Northwestern Community Development Corps

Organized Action by Students Invested in Society

Phi Beta Sigma

Project Wildcat

Residence Hall Association

Residential College Board

Rotaract Club of Northwestern University

Special Olympics

Student Blood Services

The Best
& Worst

The Ten BEST Things About Northwestern

1	Proximity to Chicago
2	Dillo Day
3	The Lakefill
4	Bright and compassionate professors
5	Well-rounded students
6	Reading Week
7	On-campus speakers
8	Dance Marathon
9	Smack in the middle of the dining capital of the North Shore
10	Medill School of Journalism and Theatre Program

The Ten **Worst** Things About Northwestern

1 Winter in Chicago

2 Dorky guys

3 The expense of living in Evanston

4 Dining hall food

5 Sub-par athletics

6 Teaching assistants

7 Suffering social scene

8 Town-gown relations

9 Norris University Center

10 Pressure to succeed

Visiting

The Lowdown On...
Visiting

Hotel Information:

Best Western University Plaza

1501 Sherman Ave.,
(847) 491-6400
www.bwuniversityplaza.com
Distance from Campus:
Less than one mile
Price Range: $85–$100

Hilton Garden Inn

1818 Maple Ave.
(847) 475-6400
www.hgievanston.com
Distance from Campus:
Less than one mile
Price Range: $140–$150

The Homestead
1625 Hinman Ave.
(847) 475-3300
www.thehomestead.net
Distance from Campus:
Less than one mile
Price Range: $100–$250

Hotel Orrington
1710 Orrington Ave.
(847) 866-8700
www.hotelorrington.com
Distance from Campus:
Less than one mile
Price Range: $110–$150

Take a Campus Virtual Tour

www.ugadm.northwestern.edu/tour

Schedule a Group Information Session or Interview

Northwestern information sessions are 45 minutes long, and reservations are not necessary unless a group of 10 or more will be attending. Check out the Admissions Office visiting site at *www.ugadm.northwestern.edu/freshman/visiting,* and click on "Information Sessions," or call (847) 491-7271 for session times, to set up reservations, or to get the most up-to-date information.

Campus Tours

Tours are given daily (except during the month of April) and last about one and a half hours. Groups of ten or more need to make reservations by contacting the Office of Undergraduate Admission at (847) 491-7271 to make reservations. Tours leave from the Office of Undergraduate Admission, which is at 1801 Hinman Avenue.

Overnight Visits

Individual overnight visits are open to high school seniors from October–April. Depending on availability, Northwestern will provide accommodations with a student host in a residence hall. Arrangements should be made through the Admissions Office by calling (847) 491-7271, or check out their Web site at *www. ugadm.northwestern.edu/freshman/visiting/#visits* Reservations should be arranged at least one month in advance.

Directions to Campus

Driving from the North

- Take the Edens Expressway (I-94) to Dempster Street.
- Take the eastbound Dempster Street exit.
- Follow Dempster Street east to Hinman Avenue in Evanston.
- Turn left (north) on Hinman.
- The Office of Undergraduate Admission is at the corner of Clark and Hinman (1801 Hinman Avenue).

Driving from the South

- Take the Tri-State Tollway (I-294) or Edens Expressway (I-94) to Dempster Street.
- Take the eastbound Dempster Street exit.
- Follow Dempster Street east to Hinman Avenue in Evanston.
- Turn left (north) on Hinman.
- The Office of Undergraduate Admission is at the corner of Clark and Hinman (1801 Hinman Avenue).

Words to Know

Academic Probation – A suspension imposed on a student if he or she fails to keep up with the school's minimum academic requirements. Those unable to improve their grades after receiving this warning can face dismissal.

Beer Pong/Beirut – A drinking game involving cups of beer arranged in a pyramid shape on each side of a table. The goal is to get a ping pong ball into one of the opponent's cups by throwing the ball or hitting it with a paddle. If the ball lands in a cup, the opponent is required to drink the beer.

Bid – An invitation from a fraternity or sorority to 'pledge' (join) that specific house.

Blue-Light Phone – Brightly-colored phone posts with a blue light bulb on top. These phones exist for security purposes and are located at various outside locations around most campuses. In an emergency, a student can pick up one of these phones (free of charge) to connect with campus police or a security escort.

Campus Police – Police who are specifically assigned to a given institution. Campus police are typically not regular city officers; they are employed by the university in a full-time capacity.

Club Sports – A level of sports that falls somewhere between varsity and intramural. If a student is unable to commit to a varsity team but has a lot of passion for athletics, a club sport could be a better, less intense option. Even less demanding, intramural (IM) sports often involve no traveling and considerably less time.

Cocaine – An illegal drug. Also known as "coke" or "blow," cocaine often resembles a white crystalline or powdery substance. It is highly addictive and dangerous.

Common Application – An application with which students can apply to multiple schools.

Course Registration – The period of official class selection for the upcoming quarter or semester. Prior to registration, it is best to prepare several back-up courses in case a particular class becomes full. If a course is full, students can place themselves on the waitlist, although this still does not guarantee entry.

Division Athletics – Athletic classifications range from Division I to Division III. Division IA is the most competitive, while Division III is considered to be the least competitive.

Dorm – A dorm (or dormitory) is an on-campus housing facility. Dorms can provide a range of options from suite-style rooms to more communal options that include shared bathrooms. Most first-year students live in dorms. Some upperclassmen who wish to stay on campus also choose this option.

Early Action – An application option with which a student can apply to a school and receive an early acceptance response without a binding commitment. This system is becoming less and less available.

Early Decision – An application option that students should use only if they are certain they plan to attend the school in question. If a student applies using the early decision option and is admitted, he or she is required and bound to attend that university. Admission rates are usually higher among students who apply through early decision, as the student is clearly indicating that the school is his or her first choice.

Ecstasy – An illegal drug. Also known as "E" or "X," ecstasy looks like a pill and most resembles an aspirin. Considered a party drug, ecstasy is very dangerous and can be deadly.

Ethernet – An extremely fast Internet connection available in most university-owned residence halls. To use an Ethernet connection properly, a student will need a network card and cable for his or her computer.

Fake ID – A counterfeit identification card that contains false information. Most commonly, students get fake IDs with altered birthdates so that they appear to be older than 21 (and therefore of legal drinking age). Even though it is illegal, many college students have fake IDs in hopes of purchasing alcohol or getting into bars.

Frosh – Slang for "freshman" or "freshmen."

Hazing – Initiation rituals administered by some fraternities or sororities as part of the pledging process. Many universities have outlawed hazing due to its degrading, and sometimes dangerous, nature.

Intramurals (IMs) – A popular, and usually free, sport league in which students create teams and compete against one another. These sports vary in competitiveness and can include a range of activities—everything from billiards to water polo. IM sports are a great way to meet people with similar interests.

Keg – Officially called a half-barrel, a keg contains roughly 200 12-ounce servings of beer.

LSD – An illegal drug, also known as acid, this hallucinogenic drug most commonly resembles a tab of paper.

Marijuana – An illegal drug, also known as weed or pot; along with alcohol, marijuana is one of the most commonly-found drugs on campuses across the country.

Major –The focal point of a student's college studies; a specific topic that is studied for a degree. Examples of majors include physics, English, history, computer science, economics, business, and music. Many students decide on a specific major before arriving on campus, while others are simply "undecided" until declaring a major. Those who are extremely interested in two areas can also choose to double major.

Meal Block – The equivalent of one meal. Students on a meal plan usually receive a fixed number of meals per week. Each meal, or "block," can be redeemed at the school's dining facilities in place of cash. Often, a student's weekly allotment of meal blocks will be forfeited if not used.

Minor – An additional focal point in a student's education. Often serving as a complement or addition to a student's main area of focus, a minor has fewer requirements and prerequisites to fulfill than a major. Minors are not required for graduation from most schools; however some students who want to explore many different interests choose to pursue both a major and a minor.

Mushrooms – An illegal drug. Also known as "'shrooms," this drug resembles regular mushrooms but is extremely hallucinogenic.

Off-Campus Housing – Housing from a particular landlord or rental group that is not affiliated with the university. Depending on the college, off-campus housing can range from extremely popular to non-existent. Students who choose to live off campus are typically given more freedom, but they also have to deal with possible subletting scenarios, furniture, bills, and other issues. In addition to these factors, rental prices and distance often affect a student's decision to move off campus.

Office Hours – Time that teachers set aside for students who have questions about coursework. Office hours are a good forum for students to go over any problems and to show interest in the subject material.

Pledging – The early phase of joining a fraternity or sorority, pledging takes place after a student has gone through rush and received a bid. Pledging usually lasts between one and two semesters. Once the pledging period is complete and a particular student has done everything that is required to become a member, that student is considered a brother or sister. If a fraternity or a sorority would decide to "haze" a group of students, this initiation would take place during the pledging period.

Private Institution – A school that does not use tax revenue to subsidize education costs. Private schools typically cost more than public schools and are usually smaller.

Prof – Slang for "professor."

Public Institution – A school that uses tax revenue to subsidize education costs. Public schools are often a good value for in-state residents and tend to be larger than most private colleges.

Quarter System (or Trimester System) – A type of academic calendar system. In this setup, students take classes for three academic periods. The first quarter usually starts in late September or early October and concludes right before Christmas. The second quarter usually starts around early to mid–January and finishes up around March or April. The last academic quarter, or "third quarter," usually starts in late March or early April and finishes up in late May or Mid-June. The fourth quarter is summer. The major difference between the quarter system and semester system is that students take more, less comprehensive courses under the quarter calendar.

RA (Resident Assistant) – A student leader who is assigned to a particular floor in a dormitory in order to help to the other students who live there. An RA's duties include ensuring student safety and providing assistance wherever possible.

Recitation – An extension of a specific course; a review session. Some classes, particularly large lectures, are supplemented with mandatory recitation sessions that provide a relatively personal class setting.

Rolling Admissions – A form of admissions. Most commonly found at public institutions, schools with this type of policy continue to accept students throughout the year until their class sizes are met. For example, some schools begin accepting students as early as December and will continue to do so until April or May.

Room and Board – This figure is typically the combined cost of a university-owned room and a meal plan.

Room Draw/Housing Lottery – A common way to pick on-campus room assignments for the following year. If a student decides to remain in university-owned housing, he or she is assigned a unique number that, along with seniority, is used to determine his or her housing for the next year.

Rush – The period in which students can meet the brothers and sisters of a particular chapter and find out if a given fraternity or sorority is right for them. Rushing a fraternity or a sorority is not a requirement at any school. The goal of rush is to give students who are serious about pledging a feel for what to expect.

Semester System – The most common type of academic calendar system at college campuses. This setup typically includes two semesters in a given school year. The fall semester starts around the end of August or early September and concludes before winter vacation. The spring semester usually starts in mid-January and ends in late April or May.

Student Center/Rec Center/Student Union – A common area on campus that often contains study areas, recreation facilities, and eateries. This building is often a good place to meet up with fellow students; depending on the school, the student center can have a huge role or a non-existent role in campus life.

Student ID – A university-issued photo ID that serves as a student's key to school-related functions. Some schools require students to show these cards in order to get into dorms, libraries, cafeterias, and other facilities. In addition to storing meal plan information, in some cases, a student ID can actually work as a debit card and allow students to purchase things from bookstores or local shops.

Suite – A type of dorm room. Unlike dorms that feature communal bathrooms shared by the entire floor, suites offer bathrooms shared only among the suite. Suite-style dorm rooms can house anywhere from two to ten students.

TA (Teacher's Assistant) – An undergraduate or grad student who helps in some manner with a specific course. In some cases, a TA will teach a class, assist a professor, grade assignments, or conduct office hours.

Undergraduate – A student in the process of studying for his or her bachelor's degree.

ABOUT THE AUTHOR

I've always wanted to write my own book, and when College Prowler gave me the chance, I jumped at it. As a journalism student, I take pride in doing research and offering a fair, unbiased view of what Northwestern has to offer, and as a member of the campus community, I think I have a good deals of insight that some of those crusty old guides just can't offer. It's been quite the experience, and a little cathartic. I've learned about myself, and why I chose Northwestern, in the process of writing this guide to help you out. I hope you enjoyed the quirky humor and that this offers you a more holistic picture of what NU is all about. There isn't much to tell about myself, just a reminder that everyone has a story, and this school is part of mine.

I can't end this without giving my props, so here goes. Thank you, thank you, thank you to the following crazies: Mommy, Shawn, Misty, Dennis Sr. and Jr., Bryan, Nathan, Alicia, Amber, Jesse, Angie, Jason, Nathan, Emma, the Rosenbaums's, the Evanston Public Library staff, Elaine, Sumeet, Tau Delta Nu, Bob, Dinah, all my professors, and everyone at College Prowler! E-mail me with any questions.

Torea Frey
authors@collegeprowler.com

The College Prowler Big Book of Colleges

Having Trouble Narrowing Down Your Choices?

Try Going Bigger!

BIG BOOK OF COLLEGES '09
7¼" X 10", 1248 Pages Paperback
$29.95 Retail
978-1-4274-0005-5

Choosing the perfect school can be an overwhelming challenge. Luckily, our *Big Book of Colleges* makes that task a little less daunting. We've packed it with overviews of our full library of single-school guides—more than 280 of the nation's top schools—giving you some much-needed perspective on your search.

College Prowler
on the Web

Craving some electronic interaction? Check out the new and improved **CollegeProwler.com**! We've included the COMPLETE contents of more than 250 of our single-school guides on the Web—and you can gain access to all of them for just $39.95 per year!

Not only that, but non-subscribers can still view and compare our grades for each school, order books at our online bookstore, or enter our monthly scholarship contest. Don't get left in the dark when making your college decision. Let College Prowler be your guide!

Get the Jolt!

College Jolt gives you a peek behind the scenes

College Jolt is our new blog designed to hook you up with great information, funny videos, cool contests, awesome scholarship opportunities, and honest insight into who we are and what we're all about.

Check us out at ***www.collegejolt.com***

Need Help Paying For School?
Apply for our scholarship!

College Prowler awards thousands of dollars a year
to students who compose the best essays.
E-mail scholarship@collegeprowler.com for more
information, or call 1-800-290-2682.

Apply now at ***www.collegeprowler.com***

Tell Us What Life Is Really Like at Your School!

Have you ever wanted to let people know what your college is really like? Now's your chance to help millions of high school students choose the right college.

Let your voice be heard.

Check out *www.collegeprowler.com* for more info!

Need More Help?

Do you have more questions about this school? Can't find a certain statistic? College Prowler is here to help. We are the best source of college information out there. We have a network of thousands of students who can get the latest information on any school to you ASAP. E-mail us at info@collegeprowler.com with your college-related questions.

E-Mail Us Your College-Related Questions!

Check out *www.collegeprowler.com* for more details.
1-800-290-2682

Write For Us!

Get published! Voice your opinion.

Writing a College Prowler guidebook is both fun and rewarding; our open-ended format allows your own creativity free reign. Our writers have been featured in national newspapers and have seen their names in bookstores across the country. Now is your chance to break into the publishing industry with one of the country's fastest-growing publishers!

Apply now at **www.collegeprowler.com**

Contact editor@collegeprowler.com or
call 1-800-290-2682 for more details.

Pros and Cons

Still can't figure out if this is the right school for you?
You've already read through this in-depth guide;
why not list the pros and cons? It will really help
with narrowing down your decision and determining
whether or not this school is right for you.

Pros	Cons
....	....
....	....
....	....
....	....
....	....
....	....
....	....
....	....
....	....
....	....
....	....
....	....
....	....

Pros and Cons

Still can't figure out if this is the right school for you?
You've already read through this in-depth guide;
why not list the pros and cons? It will really help
with narrowing down your decision and determining
whether or not this school is right for you.

Pros	Cons
....	....
....	....
....	....
....	....
....	....
....	....
....	....
....	....
....	....
....	....
....	....
....	....
....	....

Notes

....

....

....

....

....

....

....

....

....

....

....

....

....

....

Notes

....
....
....
....
....
....
....
....
....
....
....
....
....

Notes

....

....

....

....

....

....

....

....

....

....

....

....

....

....

Notes

....

....

....

....

....

....

....

....

....

....

....

....

....

....

Notes

....

....

....

....

....

....

....

....

....

....

....

....

....

....

Notes

....
....
....
....
....
....
....
....
....
....
....
....
....
....

Notes

....

....

....

....

....

....

....

....

....

....

....

....

....

Notes

....

....

....

....

....

....

....

....

....

....

....

....

Notes

....

....

....

....

....

....

....

....

....

....

....

....

....

....

Notes

....

....

....

....

....

....

....

....

....

....

....

....

....

Notes

....

....

....

....

....

....

....

....

....

....

....

....

....

Notes

....

....

....

....

....

....

....

....

....

....

....

....

....

Notes

....

....

....

....

....

....

....

....

....

....

....

....

....

Notes

....

....

....

....

....

....

....

....

....

....

....

....

....

....

Notes

....

....

....

....

....

....

....

....

....

....

....

....

....

Notes

....

....

....

....

....

....

....

....

....

....

....

....

....

....

Notes

....

....

....

....

....

....

....

....

....

....

....

....

....

Albion College
Alfred University
Allegheny College
American University
Amherst College
Arizona State University
Auburn University
Babson College
Ball State University
Bard College
Barnard College
Bates College
Baylor University
Beloit College
Bentley College
Binghamton University
Birmingham Southern College
Boston College
Boston University
Bowdoin College
Brandeis University
Brigham Young University
Brown University
Bryn Mawr College
Bucknell University
Cal Poly
Cal Poly Pomona
Cal State Northridge
Cal State Sacramento
Caltech
Carleton College
Carnegie Mellon University
Case Western Reserve
Centenary College of Louisiana
Centre College
Claremont McKenna College
Clark Atlanta University
Clark University
Clemson University
Colby College
Colgate University
College of Charleston
College of the Holy Cross
College of William & Mary
College of Wooster
Colorado College
Columbia University
Connecticut College
Cornell University
Creighton University
CUNY Hunters College
Dartmouth College
Davidson College
Denison University
DePauw University
Dickinson College
Drexel University
Duke University
Duquesne University
Earlham College
East Carolina University
Elon University
Emerson College
Emory University
FIT
Florida State University
Fordham University

Franklin & Marshall College
Furman University
Geneva College
George Washington University
Georgetown University
Georgia Tech
Gettysburg College
Gonzaga University
Goucher College
Grinnell College
Grove City College
Guilford College
Gustavus Adolphus College
Hamilton College
Hampshire College
Hampton University
Hanover College
Harvard University
Harvey Mudd College
Haverford College
Hofstra University
Hollins University
Howard University
Idaho State University
Illinois State University
Illinois Wesleyan University
Indiana University
Iowa State University
Ithaca College
IUPUI
James Madison University
Johns Hopkins University
Juniata College
Kansas State
Kent State University
Kenyon College
Lafayette College
LaRoche College
Lawrence University
Lehigh University
Lewis & Clark College
Louisiana State University
Loyola College in Maryland
Loyola Marymount University
Loyola University Chicago
Loyola University New Orleans
Macalester College
Marlboro College
Marquette University
McGill University
Miami University of Ohio
Michigan State University
Middle Tennessee State
Middlebury College
Millsaps College
MIT
Montana State University
Mount Holyoke College
Muhlenberg College
New York University
North Carolina State
Northeastern University
Northern Arizona University
Northern Illinois University
Northwestern University
Oberlin College
Occidental College

Ohio State University
Ohio University
Ohio Wesleyan University
Old Dominion University
Penn State University
Pepperdine University
Pitzer College
Pomona College
Princeton University
Providence College
Purdue University
Reed College
Rensselaer Polytechnic Institute
Rhode Island School of Design
Rhodes College
Rice University
Rochester Institute of Technology
Rollins College
Rutgers University
San Diego State University
Santa Clara University
Sarah Lawrence College
Scripps College
Seattle University
Seton Hall University
Simmons College
Skidmore College
Slippery Rock
Smith College
Southern Methodist University
Southwestern University
Spelman College
St. Joseph's at Saint Philadelphia
St. John's University
St. Louis University
St. Olaf College
Stanford University
Stetson University
Stony Brook University
Susquehanna University
Swarthmore College
Syracuse University
Temple University
Tennessee State University
Texas A & M University
Texas Christian University
Towson University
Trinity College Connecticut
Trinity University Texas
Truman State
Tufts University
Tulane University
UC Berkeley
UC Davis
UC Irvine
UC Riverside
UC San Diego
UC Santa Barbara
UC Santa Cruz
UCLA
Union College
University at Albany
University at Buffalo
University of Alabama
University of Arizona
University of Central Florida
University of Chicago

University of Colorado
University of Connecticut
University of Delaware
University of Denver
University of Florida
University of Georgia
University of Illinois
University of Iowa
University of Kansas
University of Kentucky
University of Maine
University of Maryland
University of Massachusetts
University of Miami
University of Michigan
University of Minnesota
University of Mississippi
University of Missouri
University of Nebraska
University of New Hampshire
University of North Carolina
University of Notre Dame
University of Oklahoma
University of Oregon
University of Pennsylvania
University of Pittsburgh
University of Puget Sound
University of Rhode Island
University of Richmond
University of Rochester
University of San Diego
University of San Francisco
University of South Carolina
University of South Dakota
University of South Florida
University of Southern California
University of Tennessee
University of Texas
University of Utah
University of Vermont
University of Virginia
University of Washington
University of Wisconsin
UNLV
Ursinus College
Valparaiso University
Vanderbilt University
Vassar College
Villanova University
Virginia Tech
Wake Forest University
Warren Wilson College
Washington and Lee University
Washington University in St. Louis
Wellesley College
Wesleyan University
West Point
West Virginia University
Wheaton College IL
Wheaton College MA
Whitman College
Wilkes University
Williams College
Xavier University
Yale University

10334263R0

Made in the USA
Lexington, KY
14 July 2011